CRAFTING DEMOCRACY

CRAFTING DEMOCRACY

FIBER ARTS AND ACTIVISM

EDITED BY
Juilee Decker
AND
Hinda Mandell

RIT PRESS
ROCHESTER,
NEW YORK

Crafting Democracy: Fiber Arts and Activism

Published and distributed by:
RIT Press
90 Lomb Memorial Drive
Rochester, NY 14623-5604
http://ritpress.rit.edu

Printed in the U.S.A.
Designed by Marnie Soom
Typeset in Whitney

ISBN 978-1-939125-59-0

Library of Congress Cataloging-in-Publication Data

Names: Decker, Juilee, editor. | Mandell, Hinda, editor. | Rochester Public Library (Rochester, N.Y.), host institution.
Title: Crafting democracy : fiber arts and activism / edited by Juilee Decker and Hinda Mandell.
Description: Rochester, New York : RIT Press, [2019] | Includes index. | Issued in connection with an exhibition held in 2019 Harold Hacker Hall, Central Library of Rochester (New York) & Monroe County.
Identifiers: LCCN 2019010411 | ISBN 9781939125590 (soft cover : alk. paper)
Subjects: LCSH: Textile crafts—Political aspects—United States—Exhibitions. | Social action—United States—History—21st century.
Classification: LCC NK8812 .C73 2019 | DDC 746.0973—dc23
LC record available at https://lccn.loc.gov/2019010411

Contents

1 Foreword
Betty M. Bayer

2 Curatorial Statement
Juilee Decker and Hinda Mandell

6 Craft as DIY, Open Source Activism of the Twenty-First Century
Juilee Decker

10 Threading Craft and Activism: Reflections from a Tailor's Granddaughter
Hinda Mandell

15 Aftershock: Curating Resistance in the Trump Era
Beth McLaughlin

22 Democracy Sandwich: Enacting Gender and Resisting Injustice in Art Quilting / Alena Amato Ruggerio

27 Museums, Textiles, and the Everyday
Kate Bonansinga

32 The Kudzu Project: Vinebombing Virginia's Confederate Monuments
Margo Smith

39 Works in the Exhibition

113 Afterword: Spinning Material Messages
Sarah Parrish

115 Acknowledgments

117 Image Credits

118 Index

Foreword

Betty M. Bayer

Craft. Is there a more apt word to press the art of democracy into service? I cannot think of one, especially in light of Juilee Decker and Hinda Mandell's curated exhibit *Crafting Democracy*.

Noun and verb, *craft*'s earliest meaning rests on four pillars: strength, power, force, and virtue; as a verb, *craft* means to construct skillfully. Craft's early synonymity with art recalls intellectual power and skill as source and effect. Therein we find at least one etymological thread of art and craft's shared status and their tendency to compel periodic crossover. It's the crossovers that may prove the more telling of this exhibit of fiber-based craft activism post the US's 2016 presidential election. Every thread, fiber, weave, and stitch reinvents art and craft as democracy's warp and weft—needling, in significant ways, relations of gender, race, class, and justice.

Over thirty pieces compose this exhibit, evoking more than thirty ways to resee and rethink, question, and imagine anew how to thread living here together through the eye of democracy. Textiles, as the artists note, offer "models of complex abstract systems," "objects made to do a job," metaphors for unraveling systems and locating in the tangle of so many strands ways to redo order, to be touched by embodied labor. We can feel the power of resistance to act, hear the sounds of opposition, and witness democracy on the move. After all, that is also the very meaning of craft—a vessel to carry us from one place to another.

Betty M. Bayer is professor of women's studies at Hobart and William Smith Colleges and recently served as president of the board of directors of the National Women's Hall of Fame. She has written on wonder and enchantment, and currently is working on a history of the 1956 book *When Prophecy Fails*, entitled *Revelation or Revolution? Cognitive Dissonance and Persistent Longing in an Age Psychological.*

Crafting Democracy: Fiber Arts and Activism Curatorial Statement

Juilee Decker, PhD
jdgsh@rit.edu
@RITmuse

Hinda Mandell, PhD
hbmgpt@rit.edu
@crochetactivism

In the summer of 2018, migrant family members, who had been separated from each other by federal authorities while seeking asylum at the American border, were being reunited. These family units were literally getting stitched back together, as children, babies, parents, and siblings were returned into a familial embrace. But for the youngest children, it did not feel familiar. The seams of their reunion, ordered by the US Department of Justice, could not conceal that the fabric of their family was ripped apart. The headline of a July 2018 *New York Times* article declares, "As Migrant Families Are Reunited, Some Children Don't Recognize Their Mothers."[1]

Considering the gravity of these families' situations, it's worth asking what role—beyond metaphorical symbolism—fiber-based craft activism can play in a democracy whose laws and moral center are tested during a presidential administration that has driven a resistance movement to speak out—and craft—against new government policies curtailing human and civil rights. As the artwork and companion catalogue in this exhibition, *Crafting Democracy: Fiber Arts and Activism*, make clear, craft is fundamentally a personal representation that draws upon creative forces through handcraft to voice dissent, express hope, critique the curtailment of civil rights, and restore dignity to the human experience. Craft, therefore, represents a texturized voice that can be seen—and heard in the symbolic sense. Fiber, with its plush textures and vibrant colors, with its resonant metaphorical

1. Miriam Jordan, Katie Benner, Ron Nixon, and Caitlin Dickerson, "As Migrant Families Are Reunited, Some Children Don't Recognize Their Mothers," *New York Times*, July 10, 2018, https://www.nytimes.com/2018/07/10/us/politics/trump-administration-catch-and-release-migrants.html.

attributes (consider the "social fabric"), lends itself lushly as a platform for expression and critique.

The origins of the catalogue and exhibition can be traced to 2016 when Hinda Mandell began to engage politically with yarn as a craft activist during the presidential campaign between Hillary Clinton and Donald Trump. Mandell is also the editor of *Crafting Dissent: Handicraft as Protest from the American Revolution to the Pussyhats* (Rowman & Littlefield). She sought out a museum studies scholar and curator to bring to life an exhibit featuring fiber arts that comment upon a contentious and divisive political climate in the immediate aftermath of the 2016 presidential election. In art historian and author Juilee Decker, Mandell found a socially conscious and engaged curator to join forces with and with whom to craft a shared vision.

Though *Crafting Democracy: Fiber Arts and Activism* reflects strikingly contemporary issues, the curators were able to take the necessary time over the course of two years to develop an exhibition, catalogue, and slate of activities to bring the project—a crafty intervention of sorts—to its intended audience, the community of Rochester, New York. Both Susan B. Anthony and Frederick Douglass called Rochester home, engaged in some of their most impactful work as leaders of the suffragist and abolitionist movements while residents of this city, and are buried at Mount Hope Cemetery in Rochester. The themes of democracy, activism, social justice, and human rights have unique local roots in Rochester historically; but this project also publicized the call for art and craftwork internationally, since the effects of the 2016 presidential election had a global reach. One of the core criteria was that submissions had to be created from 2015 onward, to capture a creative moment coinciding with the 2016 presidential campaign (kicked off in 2015), the election, and its immediate aftermath. More than one hundred submissions were received, with about thirty percent of submitted works selected for the exhibit. The goal in the jurying process was to explore the lasting and unfinished legacies of renowned abolitionist and suffragist icons in the United States, as well as the role of craft activism in contemporary life.

The notion of everyday life loomed large as possible venues were considered for the exhibit. While there are many galleries and exhibit spaces to choose from on campus and off, the curators were committed to making this exhibit available to the public in an inviting venue with a low barrier of entry. In short, it called for a democratic space. Enter the Harold Hacker Hall of the Central Library of Rochester & Monroe County, where Juilee Decker had worked with a team of curators and scholars to mount an exhibit on New York's suffrage centennial in 2017. The library and its exhibit team made welcome collaborators, meeting regularly with the curators at the central branch to discuss the show and corollary programming.

Works in this exhibition demonstrate how objects of material culture can provoke and engage members of the public, including those of marginalized identities, as productive tools in deliberative democracies; craft can also amplify lesser heard voices through the process of making. In order to draw attention to links between the local and the global, the work of Rochester-area residents of all ages will be on display, along with that of art activists, or craftivists, from across the US and abroad who use the traditional tools of craft (yarn, thread, textiles) to make statements about sociopolitical, cultural, and economic issues that have engaged them, prompting them to turn to craft as a pathway to positive change and the pursuit of social justice.

Themes quickly crystallized from the body of work selected for this exhibition: the 2016 election, identity politics, polarization, the endless march toward progress and recognition of self-worth, and resilience and hope. Along the way, it became clear how continuously threatened citizenship status, democratic participation, and equality remain. The media and techniques represented include crocheted, woven, quilted, cross-stitched, and knitted objects, using yarn, thread, and fabric, all speaking to the ways in which fiber—when controlled, constrained, tamed, and harnessed, or loosened, freed, unraveled, and unbound—is the ideal medium of and for activism. The works on view represent the creative and artistic output of those who make it their life's business to "craft democracy." By doing so, these artists teach us how to open our hearts and minds to the diversity of paths available in this democracy to be actively engaged as we march toward progress. Their works offer a range of expression that demonstrates how fiber, art, and activism can be employed to raise concerns, to fight injustice in sociocultural, political, and economic issues. As we now turn our attention to the 2020 presidential election campaign, we also look toward the youth in the US as the torchbearers of activist movements, as we tie together our dreams and missions for a more inclusive world.

Crafting Democracy: Fiber Arts & Activism is on view August 1, 2019 through October 25, 2019 in the Anthony Mascioli Gallery, on the first floor of the Rundel Memorial Library Building, Central Library of Rochester & Monroe County.

Craft as DIY, Open-Source Activism of the Twenty-First Century

Juilee Decker

Craft carries purpose, meaning, and context in domestic and institutional spheres, whether serving as utilitarian necessity or activist embodiment. Consider its role in the reform work of the past century, from woman suffrage to the women's movement of the 1960s, 1970s, and today. Banners, posters, and other woven, appliquéd, sewn, and stitched goods have become essential tools of the resistance, while patterns have emerged as indispensable for sowing the seeds of resistance. In fact, patterns serve as both structure and system, framework and network. They are the apparatus of resistance and serve as a do-it-yourself (DIY), open-source form of activism especially well suited for the twenty-first century. Patterns engage in that symbiotic relationship of craft and activism that calls for introspection and empathy, as stated by Betsy Greer, who popularized the term *craftivism*: "a way of looking at life where voicing opinions through creativity makes your voice stronger, your compassion deeper & your quest for justice more infinite."[1]

There's no question that activist works, including those featured in the exhibition *Crafting Democracy*, tap into a DIY spirit, a do-it-yourself approach to adopting, if not crafting, political power. For example, in the wake of the 2016 US presidential election, Berkeley-based artist Stephanie Syjuco had designed and distributed flyers for a November protest before turning her attention to creating a series of banners for the Trump era. She made them accessible on a Google drive; her PDF entitled *Making Fabric Protest Banners: Tips + Tricks* peppered the

1 *Craftivism*, combining craft and activism in a symbiotic relationship, surfaced in the early twenty-first century and was brought to a wider audience. See Betsy Greer, "Craftivism," http://craftivism.com/definition/.

internet. In this manifesto of sorts, Syjuco outlined her predilection for the analog as opposed to the digital: "There's something about wanting to dig into the materiality of *stuff* and have a direct hand in a work's creation that is hard to argue against. . . . The slowed-down timeframe of having to actually *make and sew something* forced me to spend more time thinking about what it was that I was arguing for in the imagery and message of the work."[2] A second example is the Pussyhat Project, the movement to adorn human beings with knitted caps, hats, or beanies as a political statement and form of resistance. Created by Krista Su, Jayna Zweiman, and Kat Coyle, the Pussyhat Project made its debut en masse in conjunction with the Women's March (in Washington, DC) on the weekend following the presidential inauguration in January 2017.[3]

In addition to being DIY, practices such as Syjuco's protest pattern book and the Pussyhat Project engage in the "share culture" of the post-digital age. Patterns for banners and hats function as an open-source medium that, like its software cognate, is made freely available, and may be redistributed and modified. In a software context, digital files function as a source code of sorts—the textual annotations that offer back-end language for front-end, visible results. The patterns are like source code: they, too, are freely available and offer instructions as to how to proceed, allowing for direct use or modification as craftivists see fit.

To draw further connections between coding and crafting, consider the characteristics the two media share. The intent in comparing coding and knitting, for example, is to demonstrate how the digital and the analog are interlaced and how they are equally important to craft and activism.

In terms of craft, and more specifically knitting, in relationship to coding,[4] four concepts merit discussion. First, knitting—with its flat and round stitches—simulates the 1s and 0s of binary code. Second, craft, and

2 Stephanie Syjuco, *Making Fabric Protest Banners: Tips + Tricks*, 2016, 3. Available with templates: https://drive.google.com/drive/folders/0B6g_dTRVOZg6eH-hTU0pvTHBDejQ.

3 Pussyhat Project, https://www.pussyhatproject.com/our-story.

4 I am grateful to Hinda Mandell for mentioning that she had read about connections between knitting and coding. Her comment, as we were discussing a draft of my essay, pointed me to the internet, where I uncovered a few references, including: Kate Buckner, "How Knitting Is Like Coding," January 2, 2015, https://medium.com/@eishande/how-knitting-is-like-coding-57a5e0880a39; Christina Koch, "The Computer Science of Knitting," February 6, 2017, https://christinalk.github.io/blog/2017/02/06/knitting-programming. While I have borrowed from Koch here, many connections can be made between pattern-based work—even recipes—and coding and computer science.

in particular knitting, involves an abbreviated language and definitional terms. The letter *P* means "purl," but in coding it means "paragraph." Each of these disciplines has a prescribed vocabulary of terms that facilitate particular actions. Third, knitting and programming both involve loops, series of instructions that are repeated until a certain criterion (length, quantity, aesthetic) is met. Fourth, patterns of all kinds—beyond needle arts—require comment, just as code does. Did the pattern yield the intended result? Does the number of rows create a shape that fits one's head so that the brim doesn't cover too much of the face? Is there anything that should be noted on the instructions so that when the pattern is used again, the adjustments made this time can be carried forward? Just as such notes might be scribbled, even in shorthand form, conveniently and easily on a knitting pattern, in its digital variant, the same holds true when a coder makes a textual note in the source to append information that doesn't need to be interpreted by the computer, only by other humans reading the code. Like the (analog) handwritten note on my pattern, the source code functions as a (digital) sticky note for future reference.

Access to the source code—that is, access to the pattern as the undergirding of process—fosters replication and innovation through copycat re-creations as well as variations inspired by the original. Transmitted via text, social media, email, and the internet writ large, the patterns can serve as activism in the age of the digital. Moreover, the simplicity in the patterns (not suggesting that they are simple, but that they lay an integral, structural foundation upon which to build) draws attention to the materials and the maker's manual labor with the goal of fostering participation from many—rather than a select, educated, enfranchised few—in contributing to a broader movement.

As digital surrogates of material manifestations, patterns like those mentioned earlier also serve analog aims through the tactility of their output—taking shape through the employ of fabric, thread, yarn, pulp, and other media. Both the patterns and their products blur the boundaries between fiber and nonfiber. In this context, they also dissolve the hierarchy of artistic media, where textiles and fiber have occupied a low rank in comparison to other materials in the fine arts, much like pencil (in juxtaposition to paint) and clay (in contrast to bronze).

Both the pattern and its product—from its conception and residence on a Google drive to its download (by the user) or sharing on social media, and finally its embodiment in the created form—are, in my reading, forms of craftivism. The initial instance and its mixing, adaptation, use, and reuse all contribute to both craft and activism, as do the creation and display of banners and beanies. The parity of pattern and product bears witness to the capacity we have, as a global community, to craft democracy.

Juilee Decker, PhD, is an associate professor of museum studies at Rochester Institute of Technology. In her research and practice, she seeks ways to facilitate dialogues between communities and the objects, spaces, places, and practices that they hold dear. Decker serves on several committees of the American Alliance of Museums and is a past board member of the National Susan B. Anthony Museum and House. She earned her PhD from the joint program in Art History and Museum Studies at Case Western Reserve University and the Cleveland Museum of Art.

Threading Craft and Activism: Reflections from a Tailor's Granddaughter

Hinda Mandell

For me, fiber is life. For a very long time (whether a decade or more, I am not sure), I have tied around my wrist some type of fibrous element that I wear until it's threadbare or I'm ready to snip its material to replace it with a new one. The thread or yarn may be made of wool, cotton, silk, or a synthetic material; it may be braided or wrapped or simply tied in an overhand knot. It's chosen for the color and texture that I find alluring, a reminder of life itself: moments of vitality, comfort, softness, but also elements of weakness, degradation, collapse, discard. It is the memory of my grandpa that has brought me to this quiet tradition. I engage in it by myself. Alone.

Martin Waysdorf, my mother's father, was a Polish-trained tailor who fled the country of his birth in 1939 as the Germans invaded Poland. He didn't realize then that he'd never see his family again, nor could he have imagined the horrors of the Holocaust that decimated his family and fellow Jews. Martin found temporary refuge in Panama, where his in-laws resided, and ultimately settled in Chicago in 1945, where he met my grandmother, Rose, a native Chicagoan. Together they raised three children. The oldest was my mom.

When I think about my grandpa, I first remember his near-constant five o'clock shadow and the glass of Coca-Cola that accompanied him everywhere. But I also think about his view of America as offering a potential for renewal from his experience as an immigrant fleeing war and how he made a living, even if a modest one, through the shop that he built on the far west side of Chicago: Austin Cleaners and Tailors, named for the neighborhood in which it resided. The shop contained the tools of his trade: spools of thread, bolts of fabric, needles, scissors, sewing machines. It was also a site of democratic ideals: not only did its operation (and a six-day workweek, every day from 7 a.m. to 7 p.m.) bring my grandfather into a mid-twentieth-century working-class American life, but it also was a micro melting pot. For more than two decades, my grandfather worked alongside a tailor and his son from Mexico City, whom he sponsored so they could live with their families in Chicago. Since my grandfather spent six years in Panama, Spanish was the shop's language among the tailors as they cut patterns for suits and dresses.[1]

For twenty-six years, my grandfather ran the Austin neighborhood shop. While he was no doubt proud of his craftsmanship, it was a profession—not a calling. My mom once told me the story about when, as a teenager, she asked her dad if he liked being a tailor. "Like it?" he yelled, my mom describing fire bursting from his green and hazel-speckled eyes. "What does 'liking' have to do with it?" The act of creating something from cloth involved his artful touch, but the demands of his job and the expectations to provide for his family meant that fiber was not a means of creative application. His outburst at my mother's query demonstrated the insurmountable gap between passion and productivity. He did not love what he did for a living, because it was task-oriented work—not his "life's work."

Since my grandfather died when I was thirteen years old, I never had the chance to have a conversation about his tailoring business, and my love of fiber, thread, and yarn grew years after his death. But these days, I do wonder what he'd think of the craftivist movements that have exploded in response to the 2016 presidential election and the administration of President Donald J. Trump.

1 I would like to extend gratitude to my aunt, the law professor Susan Waysdorf, for her research into my grandfather's tailoring business that resulted in the article, "Two Tailors: The Pursuit of Racial Justice in 1970s Chicago," *University of the District of Columbia Law Review* 9, no. 1 (Winter 2007).

Indeed, the lead up to the election marked my foray into craft activism when—with a close friend—we adorned the statues of Frederick Douglass and Susan B. Anthony in the *Let's Have Tea* sculpture in Rochester, New York, with crocheted accessories featuring the appliquéd initials of Democratic presidential candidate Hillary Clinton. Since that first yarn intervention in October 2016, I've turned to yarn as a fibrous extension of my voice as a concerned citizen in half a dozen politically motivated craft campaigns.

My grandfather was always politically engaged, devouring his morning and afternoon newspapers, and vociferously offering an opinion that always slanted heavily left. He was known to unleash political rants to anyone (listening or not) in his immediate vicinity, even if he was not a blustery man overall. Yet sometimes I worry—as a person who engages in yarn-based activism —that he'd have thought my fibrous activities frivolous. His was a craft dictated by Old Country skill but predicated by necessity. Need a suit? Need a skirt hemmed? Require a shirt to be taken in? That was Martin's job, upon which his and his family's livelihood teetered. His tools were the means of artistic tucking, sewing, pleating—for sure—but the end result was practical, sometimes even utilitarian. How would my grandfather, who escaped death in Poland to arrive in America with the tools and skills to build a life as a small business owner, have reacted to the Pussyhats? To the subversive embroidery that lauded "Persisterhood"? To the handcrafted appliqués declaring oneself a "Nasty Woman"? To the tools of his trade becoming tools of outspoken political resistance? His life was marked by so many grave and life-altering events, from escaping Poland in 1939, living as an émigré in Panama during the war, and losing his entire family to Hitler's murderous Final Solution, to immigrating to the US after the Second World War. Democracy for him was more than a vague concept—it was life and security. Through his sacrifice, I inherited great privilege. My grandpa literally had to sew and mend his life back together as an immigrant who escaped hell. Yet I, as a third-generation American, have the liberty to view the "leisurely" activity of craft as a metaphor for life. It's that difference, in his life and my own, which makes me self-conscious that he may have thought of my craft-activist activities as little more than a glorified hobby.

In these moments of doubt, I find solace in another anecdote my mother shared, this time about when she told her father that she had learned in her 1950s grade-school classroom that America is the greatest country in the world. His fiery eyes reflected the anger in his voice: "The greatest country? Why don't you go ask your teacher what the Americans did to the Indians!" In this story I find a rage that's recognizable among the #resistance today, of which I call myself a member, even if my activism does not carry with it the fatal risks that took the lives of Martin's family members who joined the resistance in Nazi-occupied Europe. Through this second story, I am able to craft a narrative featuring my grandfather that is sympathetic to craft-based activism, and to imagine a space where he would have engaged in it alongside his granddaughter. If only our lifetimes had aligned differently.

The fiber tied around my wrist is a tribute to my grandfather—his life and all that he risked and left behind in Poland, resulting in the twists of fate that allowed me to be born in late twentieth-century America. I am not the only one who sees a symbolic connection between fiber and life. In fact, the relationship is cultural. Anthropologist Mirjam Mencej's article "Connecting Threads"[2] in the journal *Folklore* argues for the symbolic meanings of spinning fiber as a metaphor for life. According to European fairytales and folk stories, thread represents connective fibers linking those who live with those who have died.[3] She writes that "while un-spun wool bears a symbolic reference to the otherworld, spinning and its result, a thread, seem to be trademarks of an existence in this world."[4] Indeed, do we not "hang by

2 Mirjam Mencej, "Connecting Threads," *Folklore*, 48 (2011). Retrieved from http://www.folklore.ee/folklore/vol48/mencej.pdf.

3 Mencej, "Connecting Threads," 61.

4 Mencej, "Connecting Threads," 77

a thread" when in a precarious life situation? Are we not part of the "social fabric" of our community and nation? Is one's life not "cut short" by an illness or an accident? Fiber and its derivatives are part of our language to help us bridge life and death. The material itself, then, becomes a metaphor for crafting change, and for bridging family history and lived experience. I'd be delighted if you would join me in selecting your own fiber to wrap around your wrist in a way that's meaningful to your own family traditions, stories, and lore.

Hinda Mandell is associate professor in the School of Communication at Rochester Institute of Technology and is a co-editor of *Nasty Women and Bad Hombres: Gender and Race in the 2016 U.S. Presidential Election* (University of Rochester Press, 2018); the author of *Sex Scandals, Gender and Power in Contemporary American Politics* (Praeger, 2017) and co-editor of *Scandal in a Digital Age* (Palgrave Macmillan, 2016). She is editor of *Crafting Dissent: Handicraft as Protest from the American Revolution to the Pussyhats* (forthcoming with Rowman & Littlefield). Her website is omghinda.com and her Twitter account is: @hindamandell and @crochetactivism.

Aftershock: Curating Resistance in the Trump Era

Beth McLaughlin

On November 8, 2016, Donald J. Trump was elected president of the United States. This shocking outcome of a polemical election incited a wave of political protest that rippled across the globe. Angry and devastated individuals took to the streets, signed online petitions, called state legislators, and made financial contributions all to demonstrate support of women's rights, civil liberties, reproductive freedoms, and other social issues openly threatened by the newly elected administration.

Millions of others found their political voices through craft. In unprecedented numbers, legions of makers created handmade objects as potent messages of resistance. Protest banners, subversive embroidery, calligraphed declarations, and cat-eared Pussyhats became handcrafted, socially engaged rallying cries. Exceeding past norms of social action in both quantity and global reach, this groundswell of creative activity formed a wave of craft activism, also known as *craftivism.*

This surge of political craft activity was met with a powerful public response and ample media attention. Firmly planted in the post-election zeitgeist, craftivism became difficult for museums to ignore, and examples began to appear in formal exhibition spaces. Among the first was the Pussyhat—a handmade pink cap with catlike ears, symbolizing the thousands created for the Women's March on Washington on January 21, 2017, the day after President Trump's inauguration. This iconic headwear was displayed in London's Victoria and

1 The Victoria and Albert Museum's Rapid Response Collection was launched in 2015 to respond to milestone moments in design and manufacturing, illustrating through collecting activity how we live our lives today.

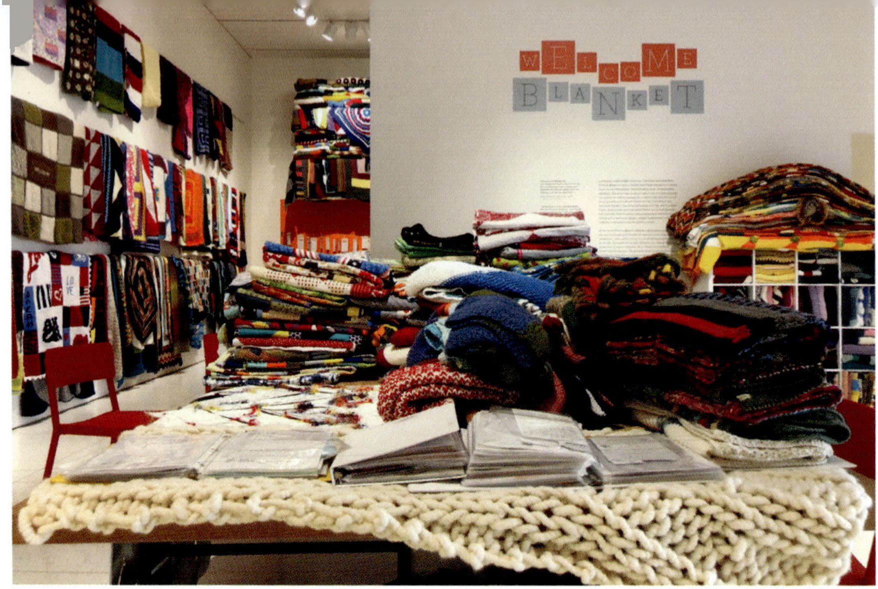

Welcome Blanket *installation at the Smart Museum, Chicago, IL. Photo: C.J. Lind*

Albert Museum in February 2017 as part of their Rapid Response Collection.[1] Later, the Smart Museum of Art in Chicago exhibited the Welcome Blanket Project, a crowd-sourced initiative that reimagined the government-proposed two-thousand-mile border wall with handcrafted blankets to probe issues of immigration and refugee resettlement.[2]

Positioning these politically charged objects within an institutional context has redefined the role of art museums, long thought to be apolitical and ageless in their approach. Since the 2016 presidential election, curators have made bold decisions as well, unapologetically developing projects that examine sociopolitical issues—many divisive and controversial. As modern institutions increasingly exhibit these provocative works, their galleries become important sites for community dialogue, reflection, and political resistance.

With more museums confronting of-the-moment

2 The Welcome Blanket Project was the second worldwide craftivism initiative founded by Jayna Zweiman. For more information, see www.welcomeblanket.org.

and rapidly unfolding issues and crises, a new set of concerns has surfaced, from managing booked gallery schedules to donor alienation to questions of quality. Programming craftivism within institutional settings is relatively new territory, with no precedents or guideposts. Museums have taken it on nonetheless, including Fuller Craft Museum in Massachusetts with its exhibition *Revolution in the Making: The Pussyhat Project*, which opened on January 21, 2018, the one-year anniversary of the first Women's March.

Shortly after the 2017 Women's March, Fuller Craft Museum began collecting Pussyhats. With an output of more than one million handmade caps, the Pussyhat Project is considered the biggest craftivism effort in modern history.[3] Few could refute its criticality to contemporary craft, and Fuller Craft Museum embarked on developing *Revolution in the Making* to mark this historical movement.

Exhibition space is at a premium for most museums. Shows are often scheduled several years in advance, leaving little room for swift curatorial response in the galleries. If *Revolution in the Making* had been required to wait its turn in the queue, there surely would have been a loss of momentum and relevancy—an unacceptable outcome for such timely, potent content. With this in mind, the exhibition was sited in a flexible space that enabled a well-timed response to the cultural phenomenon.

Other challenges arose. While museum leadership was largely supportive, *Revolution in the Making* became an institutional flashpoint for a debate about museums and neutrality. Can—and should—cultural institutions position themselves at the locus of the sociopolitical conversation? How does a museum balance social responsibility with logistical headaches, offended visitors, and a potential loss of funders? Fuller Craft's answer is that rather than operate at the margins of socially important issues, contemporary museums must square up to them

3 The Pussyhat Project was founded by Jayna Zweiman and Krista Suh, with support from Kat Coyle, to outfit those attending the Women's March on Washington with hats to make a massive visual statement of support for equality and reproductive freedoms. For more information, see www.pussyhatproject.com.

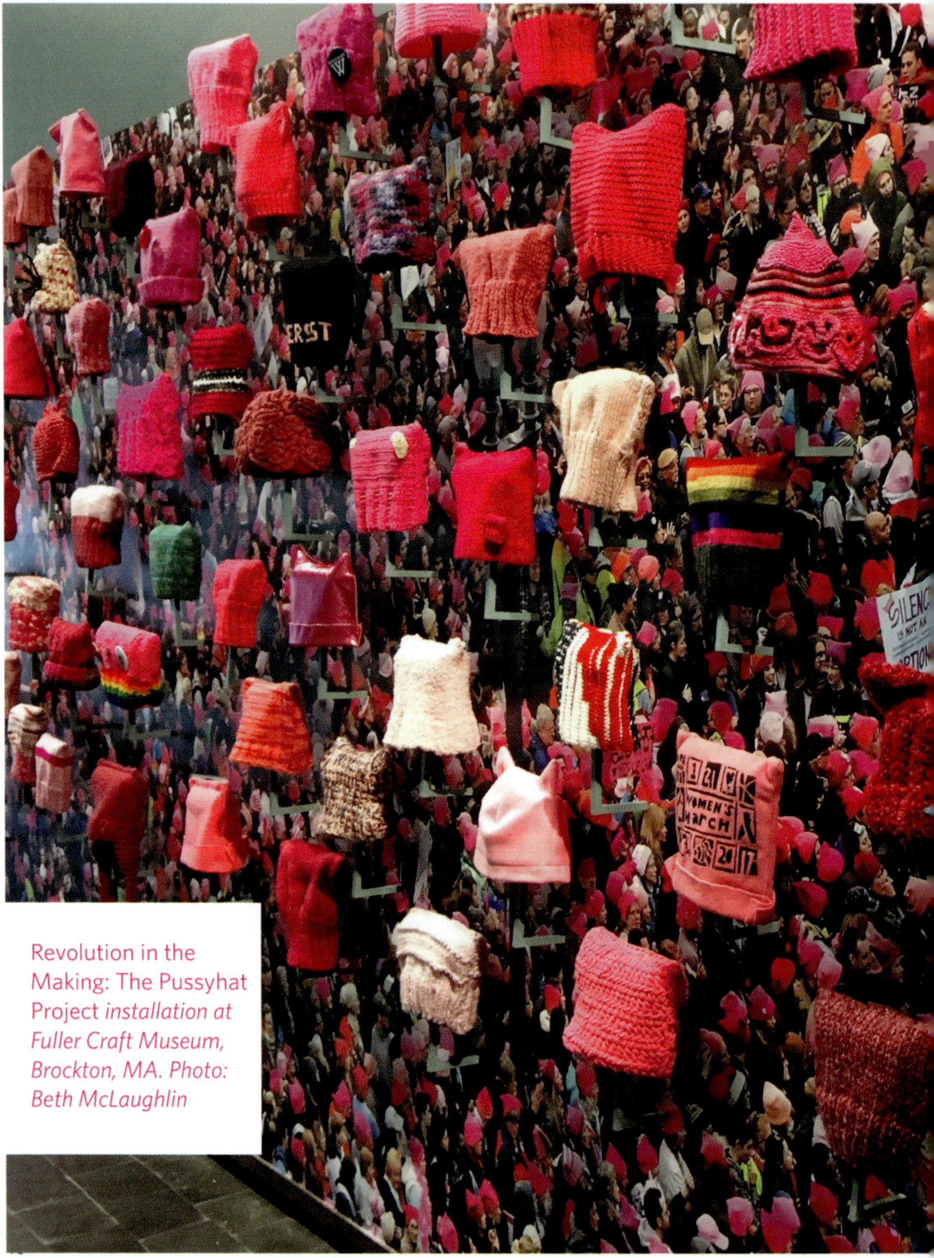

Revolution in the Making: The Pussyhat Project *installation at Fuller Craft Museum, Brockton, MA. Photo: Beth McLaughlin*

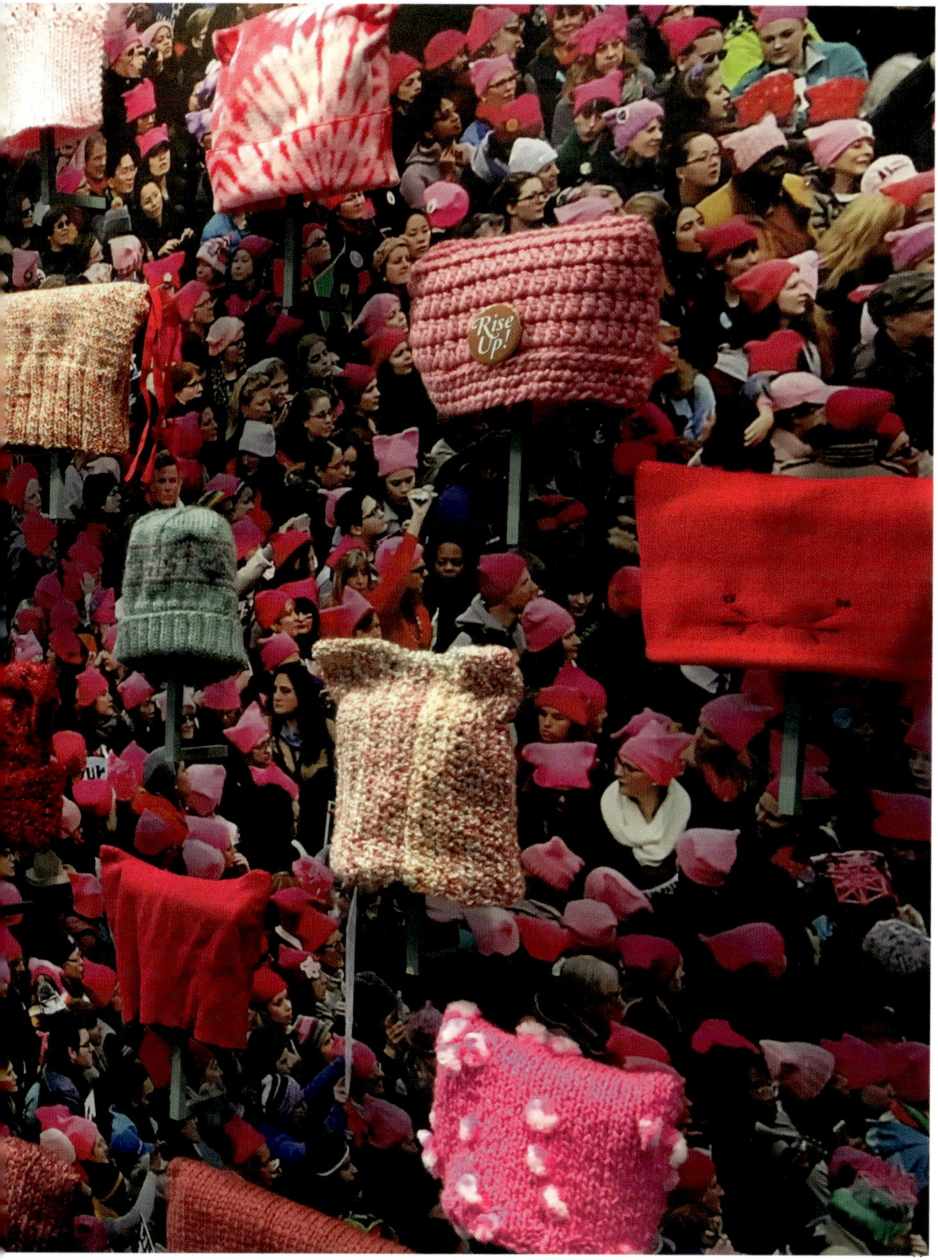
Rise Up!

and thus fulfill their missions to collect, preserve, interpret, and present objects with cultural, historical, artistic, or scientific significance.

The notion of artistic value in visual arts institutions is often tied to aesthetic achievement and evidence of technical skill. Not surprisingly, the presentation of craftivist works in museum settings has triggered a sizeable shift from these artistic frameworks to the value potential of a handmade item. In the case of the Pussyhats, meaning and intent eclipsed technical skill and aesthetic achievement, upending established notions about excellence and what it means to be a "significant object." Many of these hats were created by amateur makers, compelled by the political landscape to attempt creative activity as an outlet for rage and a response to disempowerment. At times, the outputs were sloppy and greenhorn in execution, yet no less powerful than those made by professional textile artists and no less suitable for museum display.

With the embrace of craftivism come concerns about capturing the charged ethos within a formal exhibition setting. The hushed environments of most museums, with discreet objects on pedestals protected under vitrines, seem antithetical to the electrifying conditions of the knitting circles and public protests responsible for the items. Can a curated presentation adequately convey the energy of the activist activities through which such potent objects came to life?

The development of *Revolution in the Making* included strategies to capture this stimulating spirit within a museum framework. Firsthand accounts from makers and wearers were included within the exhibition in both audio and visual formats, along with an audience participation area that prompted visitors to share their stories. Knitting workshops were held within the gallery, and a special giveaway of donated Pussyhats outfitted visitors for upcoming protests. These approaches offered fresh opportunities for discussion and continued political

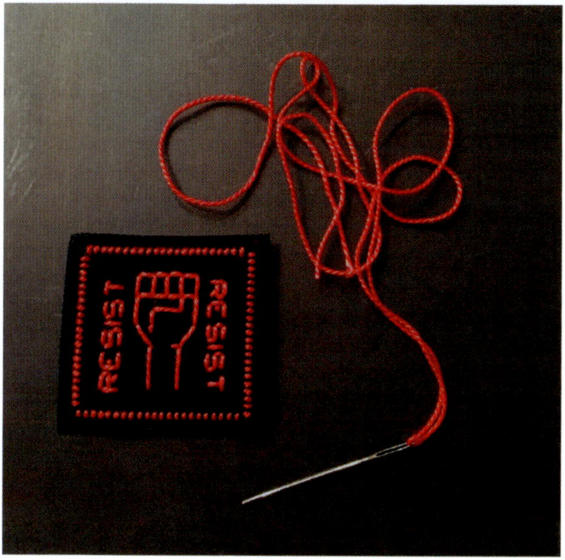

Resist *cross stitch by Shannon Downey, a.k.a. Badass Cross Stitch. Photo: Shannon Downey*

action through craft. They also established an institutional road map for developing future social projects with relevancy, respect, and vitality.

Today, global politics remain as divisive as ever, and craft artists continue to respond with works rooted in social justice and materials-based resistance.

As they navigate this shaky political ground, cultural institutions and their curators face a choice: to refrain from looking outward to the populations they serve or to engage with the aftershocks that are defining the material culture of this era.

Beth C. McLaughlin is chief curator of exhibitions and collections at Fuller Craft Museum in Brockton, Massachusetts. For over twenty-five years, Ms. McLaughlin has held leadership and curatorial positions at cultural institutions across the US, including Fuller Craft Museum, the Oakland Museum of California, and DeCordova Sculpture Park and Museum. She has been published in several national periodicals and is passionate about expanding awareness of art forms in craft-based media, promoting the makers, and exploring the transformative powers of handwork.

Democracy Sandwich: Enacting Gender and Resisting Injustice in Art Quilting

Alena Amato Ruggerio

Nearly everyone has wrapped themselves in a comforting quilt. It likely consisted of three layers—a decorative top in a geometric pattern, a thick middle batting, and a backing fabric—unified by tied knots or quilting stitches in what is known as a quilt sandwich. These traditional piecework quilts deserve great respect for their technical precision and execution of color and line. Beyond them, however, exists a world of art quilts usually constructed in the same three-layer sandwich, but meant to hang on a wall rather than cover a bed. Art quilts can be realistic and representational or abstract and fantastical. They are often embellished with myriad materials and techniques, including hand painting, inks, fused raw-edge appliqué, photographs printed on fabric, beads, crystals, overlays of tulle, thread painting, and three-dimensional objects.

Quilts are not merely utilitarian or beautiful, but are also rhetorical. In other words, quilters are communicators, engaging in a mutual process of creating meaning with their audiences. More specifically, quilters are *democratic* communicators who point their sewing needles toward creating change and enacting those changes in their own lives.

The senders of these rhetorical messages are overwhelmingly women. Men certainly do quilt, and a few (Ricky Tims and Joe Cunningham, for example) have achieved celebrity in the quilting world, in part due to their minority status. But it is women who labor to make the vast majority of quilts and who are the primary consumers of the multi-billion-dollar quilting market. Quilting offers the artists autonomy over an aspect of their lives. When working in their studios, quilters take control of their own time, their own physical space, and their own choice of messages to send through their art. In a culture that continues to undervalue women's voices, quilting provides a platform for the self-expression of silenced populations. For some, it also offers empowering economic opportunities. Women quilters design fabric lines, own quilt shops and retreat centers, instruct classes, lead guilds, write blogs and articles, organize and jury quilt shows, and curate quilt museums.

Conversely, quilting is considered a "permissible" art form for women because of its association with the domestic, the private, and the utilitarian—all of which carry connotations of inferiority in a society in which the feminine is oppressed. A quilter can have time to herself and express herself through her art as long as it is ultimately useful in the home and serves her family. This dismissal of quilting has historically provided cover for women to express political positions they would have been censured for voicing publicly, such as in the Civil War–era *Secession Quilt* by Jemima Ann Thewitts Williamson Cook, which features stitched political symbols reflecting the artist's feelings about the Union and Confederacy from the point of view of a military wife, as reported by media studies researcher Mary Rose Williams.[1] Moreover, the quilting bees of earlier generations and the round-robin quilts of today point to quilting's collaborative nature, and hence the opportunity for women to gather and discuss the dominations and resistances of their lives in spaces ignored by a culture of multiple intersecting dominations and privileges.

It is important to interrogate *which* women's lives quilting has empowered, however. Historically, white women have taken credit for competition quilts made by their slaves and servants of color. The stories of quilters

1 Mary Rose Williams, "A Reconceptualization of Protest Rhetoric: Women's Quilts as Rhetorical Forms," *Women's Studies in Communication* 17, no. 2 (1994): 20, https://login.glacier.sou.edu/login?url=https://search.ebscohost.com/login.aspx?direct=true&db=ufh&AN=14612331&site=ehost-live.

embedding messages in quilts to signal stops along the Underground Railroad remain unproven. Today, white quilters still receive disproportionate representation in the quilting magazines and museums, despite talented quilters of color, such as Alabama's Gee's Bend collective, who count among the world's finest abstract artists. It is difficult for low-income quilters to afford quilting supplies, furniture, and machines, some of which cost as much as a compact car.

Quilters of all genders and races have used this art form to interrupt injustices. The most famous example is the AIDS Memorial Quilt, which resisted the Reagan administration's inaction toward the AIDS epidemic in the 1980s. Carole Blair, professor of communication studies at the University of North Carolina, and Neil Michel, partner at Axiom Photo Design, state that the AIDS Memorial Quilt democratized public memory, allowing loved ones at all levels of needle skills to create quilt panels expressing the individuality of each life lost to AIDS.[2] Communication scholars Kevin Michael DeLuca, Christine Harold, and Kenneth Rufo argue that the AIDS Memorial Quilt makes the history of the AIDS epidemic more accessible than would a traditional public monument. In their chaotically colorful homemade tackiness, the designs on the AIDS Memorial Quilt violate the cultural expectations of morbid solemnity and instead open up a space for the makers to memorialize their dead with all the rage, passion, and creativity they choose.[3] Another democratizing aspect of the AIDS Memorial Quilt is the requirement for each panel to have the same dimensions, which approximate the measurements of a grave. As a result, both the high-status famous and those known only to their loved ones are valued equally on their quilt panels as lives lost in the AIDS epidemic.

Quilters also express their social values through quilting-based nonprofits. Quilts of Valor honors injured US veterans with patriotic blankets. Project Linus donates handmade quilts to children in homeless shelters and

2 Carole Blair and Neil Michel, "The AIDS Memorial Quilt and the Contemporary Culture of Public Commemoration," *Rhetoric & Public Affairs* 10, no. 4 (2007): 600–601.

3 Kevin Michael DeLuca, Christine Harold, and Kenneth Rufo, "Q.U.I.L.T.: A Patchwork of Reflections," *Rhetoric & Public Affairs* 10, no. 4 (2007): 642.

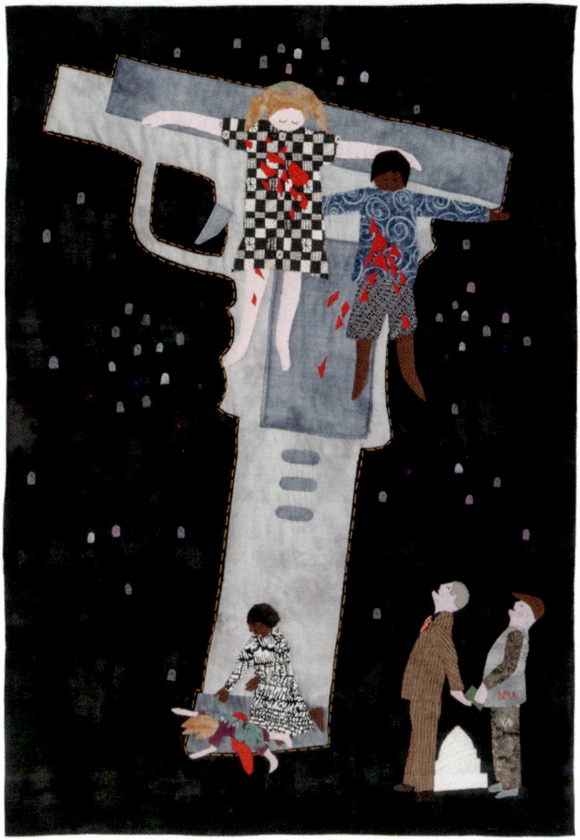

The quilt The New American Crucifix *by Nancy Lemke from 2017. Photo: Gary Connaughton*

hospitals. Days for Girls encourages quilters to sew washable menstrual pads to enable girls in Africa and India to attend school. Others make pillowcases and duffel bags for American children transitioning into foster care.

Some quilters take more controversial stands. Rhetorician Jane Amelon recounts the story of the Battered Offenders Self-Help Group, whose quilt depicting their histories as survivors of domestic violence persuaded the governor of Kentucky to grant clemency to the women for killing their abusers in self-defense.[4] The recent Studio Art Quilt Associates exhibition *Guns: Loaded Conversations* includes works with titles such as *Body Count*, *(White) Silence is Violence*, and Nancy Lemke's provocative piece, *The New American Crucifix*, depicting bleeding school children hanging as if crucified upon a handgun. Others have communicated dissent in their quilts against issues such as environmental destruction, xenophobia against immigrants, limited healthcare options and terminal diseases, Japanese internment, child labor, and violations of free speech.

Quilters are actively engaged in the public sphere, using their needle arts to participate in the democratic process, changing both social conditions and their own lives—and have done so throughout American history. Quilts draw together into their three-layer sandwich the complexities of democratic life and warm us for the task of engaging as world citizens.

4 Jane Amelon, "The Persuasive Power of a Quilt: A Study of a Women's Prison Project," *Uncoverings* 30 (2009): 77.

Alena Amato Ruggerio, PhD, is professor of communication at Southern Oregon University, a former coordinator of the SOU gender, sexuality, and women's studies program, and the organizer of two exhibitions of art quilts on her campus.

Museums, Textiles, and the Everyday

Kate Bonansinga

"I think that museums need crafts a whole lot more than crafts need museums," stated Peter Marzio (1943-2010), director of the Museum of Fine Arts, Houston, when he addressed the audience at the 2006 American Craft Council's leadership conference.[1] It was a cathartic conclusion to an oration in which Marzio reminded us that our Protestant forefathers believed artistic objects were artifacts of greed that impeded our relationship with God. Around the late nineteenth century, industry and utility were separated from the fine arts, an effect of modernism that continues to this day. As a rule, we regard useful objects with less suspicion than we regard art for art's sake. Useful objects are democratic in their intention: many of us believe that arts and crafts for all fosters the responsible and socially engaged citizens that are necessary for a successful democracy.[2] Marzio's statement refers to this belief and to the broad appeal of crafts and the decorative arts. In museum exhibitions, they bring audiences who might be skeptical of concept-driven art, but have fond memories of the quilt that covered their childhood bed or the cup that holds their morning coffee. Crafts draw crowds.

Increasing the audience at the Contemporary Arts Center (CAC) in Cincinnati, Ohio, was only one of several goals for the exhibition *Unraveled: Challenging Textile Traditions,* which was on view during the summer of 2016. I served as guest curator. The CAC was founded in 1939 and resided in various locations until its move in 2003 to the current location in an 85,000-square-foot building

1 Accessed June 25, 2018, https://craftcouncil.org/post/remembering-visionary-peter-marzio. Under Peter Marzio's direction from 1982-2010, the MFAH flourished, adding two new buildings and a sculpture garden designed by Isamu Noguchi, developing a vibrant educational outreach program, and growing its collection from 14,000 to 62,000 works of art.

2 This concept took root in the late nineteenth century. "I do not want art for a few any more than education for a few, or freedom for a few," stated William Morris (1834-1896), textile designer and social activist associated with

designed by the architect Zaha Hadid (1950–2016). It is a non-collecting museum that focuses on new developments in painting, sculpture, photography, architecture, performance art, and new media. Its core audience tends to embrace the avant-garde. I wanted to play to this audience, but also develop a new one, consisting of people with a love of textiles, from tablecloths to sweaters.

Unraveled featured nine artists, all of whom reshape previously used cloth. At least two of those nine (Kari Steihaug of Oslo, Norway, and Marie Watt of Portland, Oregon) honor the past and anonymous, collective memory.

Steihaug gathered seventy knitted pieces of clothing from friends, family members, and flea markets to be the material for *Legacies* (2006). She unraveled the garments, wound all of the yarn remnants onto industrial bobbins, and partially knitted a new sweater. Through this action, she took ownership of the memories of others to create an aggregate imagined one. Steihaug states, "Worn out knitted garments are like layers of time. The time it takes to spin the yarn, color it, knit the garment, wear it, repair it and wear it again, before it ends up in the rag pile, and my work can start. . . . I want to give concrete visual form to the relation between destruction and new creation, and the transition from one form to another."[3] The artist brings attention to unknown knitters from previous times and pays tribute to their labors.

Marie Watt, the Portland-based artist, explains, "I am interested in how blankets are objects that we take for granted, but that can have extraordinary histories. . . . Blankets are also personal to me. In my tribe—I am Seneca—and other native communities, we give blankets away to honor people for standing witness to important life events . . . they receive infants into the world and shroud us when we die." Recently Watt has organized sewing circles as a method of community building, where unorchestrated teaching transpires.[4]

the British Arts and Crafts Movement in 1878, about the time that crafts and fine art were beginning to go their separate ways. William Morris, *The Decorative Arts in their Relation to Modern Life and Progress: An Address Delivered Before the Trades' Guild of Learning* (London: Ellis and White, 1878), 30.

Kari Steihaug, Legacies, *2006, yarn, wood bobbins. Courtesy of the artist. As displayed at Contemporary Arts Center, Cincinnati, Ohio, April 22–August 14, 2016. Photo: Tony Walsh*

Foreground: Kari Steihaug, Legacies. *Background: Adrian Esparza,* Dawn, *2016, blanket, wood, nail, enamel. Courtesy of the artist. As displayed at Contemporary Arts Center, Cincinnati, Ohio, April 22–August 14, 2016. Photo: Tony Walsh*

3 Kari Steihaug, email message to author, February 2016.

4 Marie Watt, "In Conversation with Marie Watt: A New Coyote Tale," *Art Journal*, Summer 2017, 125–35.

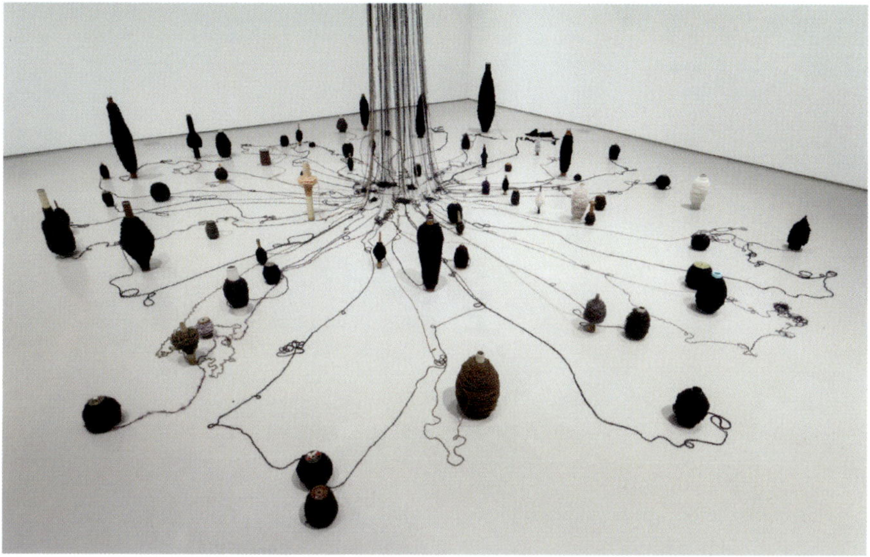

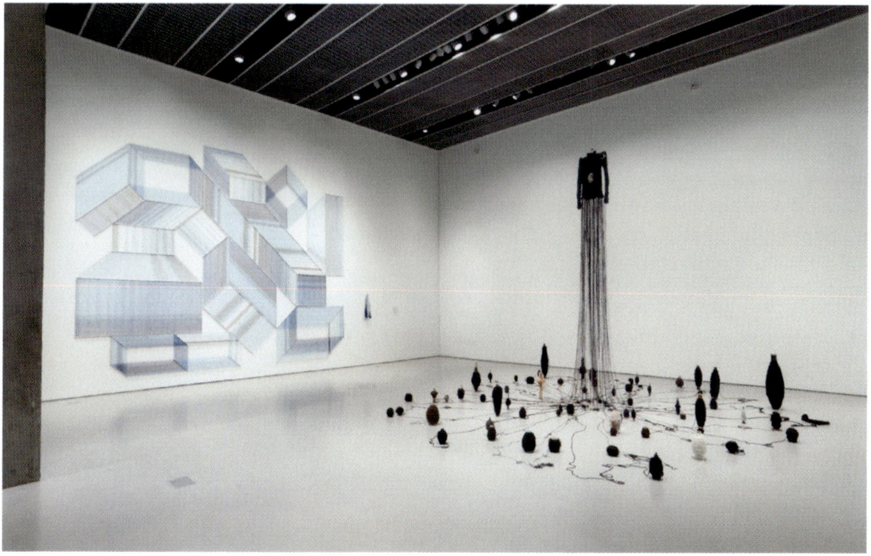

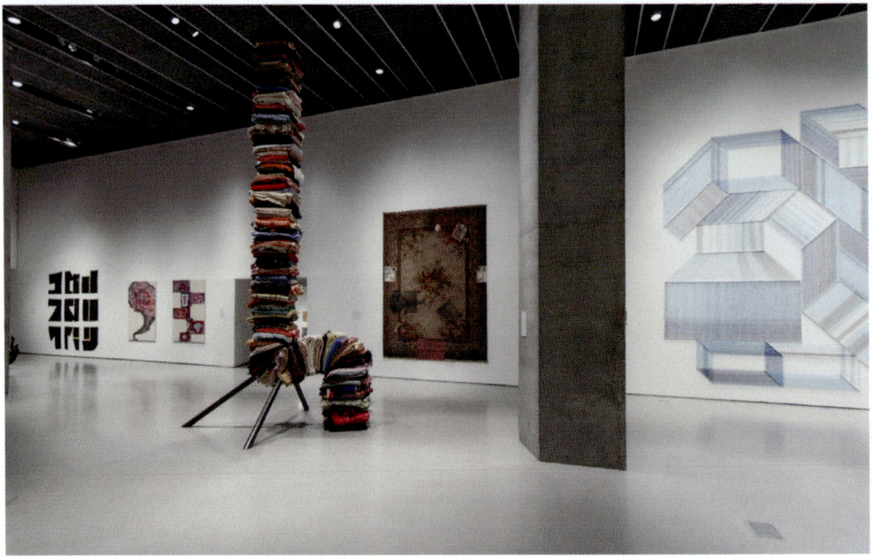

Foreground: Marie Watt, Blanket Stories: Beacon, Marker and Ohio-yo, *2016, steel armature, reclaimed blankets. Courtesy of the artist. Background left to right: Ying Kit Chan,* Convenience, *2014. Discarded bed sheets, black gesso. Courtesy of the artist. Mark R. Smith,* Peninsular, *2015, and* Trundle, *2015, textile collage on felt and textile collage on felt. Courtesy of the artist. Noel Anderson,* Black Past-iche (to be looked at farandaway; rug), *2015, rug, found materials. Courtesy of the artist. Adrian Esparza,* Dawn, *2016. Photo: Tony Walsh*

For *Unraveled*, she created a twenty-one-foot-high stack of used blankets that in its form references both Native American marker trees and totem poles, and in its material honors the formative moments in anonymous lives.

Both Steihaug and Watt harness the unique qualities of textiles to do justice to the past, to acknowledge textile makers and users who are usually unacknowledged, and to honor and create community. They reference social fabric with actual fabric.

Whether I achieved a new audience for the CAC was not determinable by the zip code data collected from visitors to the exhibit. But there was maximum enrollment in the related education programs for youth and adults, such as the two-day adult art-making workshop that encouraged participants to begin with an item of clothing representing a painful time or circumstance, deconstruct it, and from it build something new. At least one thing is clear to me: by choosing to exhibit

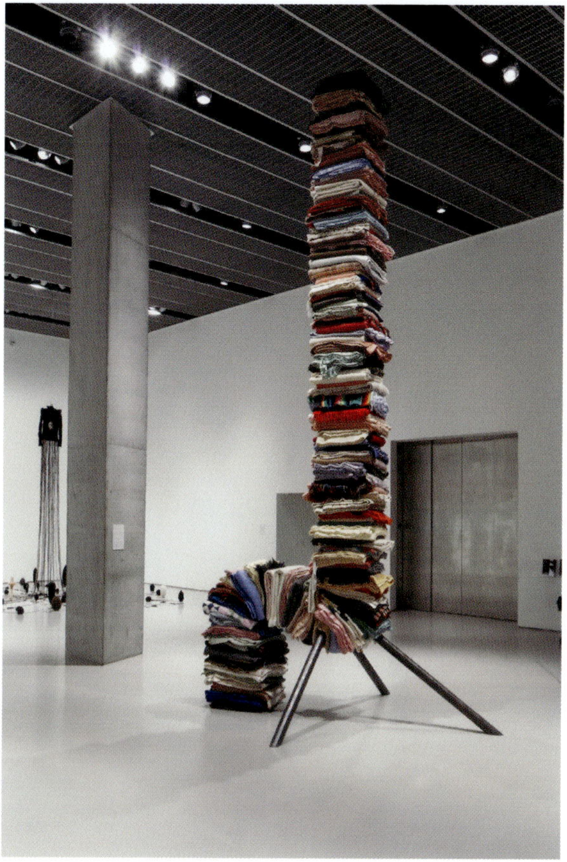

Foreground: Marie Watt, Blanket Stories: Beacon, Marker and Ohio-yo. *Background: Kari Steihaug,* Legacies. *As displayed at Contemporary Arts Center, Cincinnati, Ohio, April 22–August 14, 2016. Photo: Tony Walsh*

art created from textiles, I populated the galleries with artworks that were both tactile and idea-driven, and that harnessed the quality of craft that Peter Marzio acknowledged was invaluable to art museums—a connection to the everyday experience of everyday people who shape democracy.

Kate Bonansinga is professor and director of the School of Art in the College of Design, Architecture, Art, and Planning at the University of Cincinnati. She is interested in museums as dynamic sites for learning and in how today's artists respond to and impact their social milieu.

The Kudzu Project: Vinebombing Virginia's Confederate Monuments

Margo Smith

They say the third time is a charm, but it wasn't for us that morning. Our telescoping aluminum poles collapsed under the knitted kudzu's weight, which had increased tremendously as its leaves and vines absorbed the predawn drizzle. Unable to vault the kudzu over the Civil War soldier standing guard in front of Albemarle County Courthouse, we jettisoned the poles and scaled the base of the statue looking for a way to wrap the crafted vines around it. At that moment, four police cars pulled up to the courthouse, lights flashing. Nothing had gone according to plan, and it seemed as if the Kudzu Project was finished before it had begun. Looking up, we saw a lone strand of knitted kudzu draped over the Confederate soldier's rifle. This scrap of success would have to suffice—for now.

The Kudzu Project was founded in Charlottesville, Virginia, in 2017. Located an hour's drive from Richmond, the state capital and capital of the Confederacy during the Civil War, Charlottesville is the home of the University of Virginia and a progressive outlier in an otherwise conservative region. Charlottesville was targeted by the KKK, neo-Nazis, and other white supremacist groups protesting throughout the summer of 2017 against the proposed removal of Confederate statues. Following the violent Unite the Right rally in Charlottesville on August 11 and 12 of that year, a group of knitters devised a plan to "yarnbomb" the statues. Their inspiration came from a drawing of a statue covered in vines, titled *Defunct Monument—Racism*, by

Dave Loewenstein. One of the founders of the Kudzu Project saw the image and thought, "We could knit that," followed by the absolute conviction that the vines should be kudzu.

A non-native member of the pea family, kudzu (*Pueraria montana*) can be seen smothering vegetation along Southern roads and railways. This quick-growing, invasive plant, which blankets abandoned cars and buildings, has been called "the vine that ate the South," an epithet of unknown origin. Kudzu-covered ruins elicit romantic notions about the past. Similarly, the romanticized ideology of the Lost Cause claims that noble Confederate generals and soldiers fought the Civil War to protect states' rights rather than the institution of slavery. This rewriting of the Civil War narrative has concealed ugly historical truths in much the same way that kudzu hides whatever lies beneath it.

Statues idolizing Confederate leaders and anonymous soldiers promoted the Lost Cause mythology while also serving to intimidate African Americans. The majority of these statues were erected between 1900 and 1930 after Southern states enacted Jim Crow laws, with a second wave of monuments appearing during the civil rights movement of the 1950s and 1960s, also coinciding with the centenary of the Civil War. Frequently placed at courthouses, the statues announced that these civic spaces were aligned with the values of the Confederacy. Since the 2015 massacre of nine worshippers at the Charleston Emanuel AME Church by a white supremacist who posted photos of himself posing with the Confederate flag on social media, monuments linked to the Confederacy have come under increased scrutiny. Progressive communities like Charlottesville wish to remove them, but are hobbled by laws that protect war memorials.

Many members of the Kudzu Project had previously participated in other craftivist activities, such as knitting Pussyhats for the 2017 Women's March on Washington,

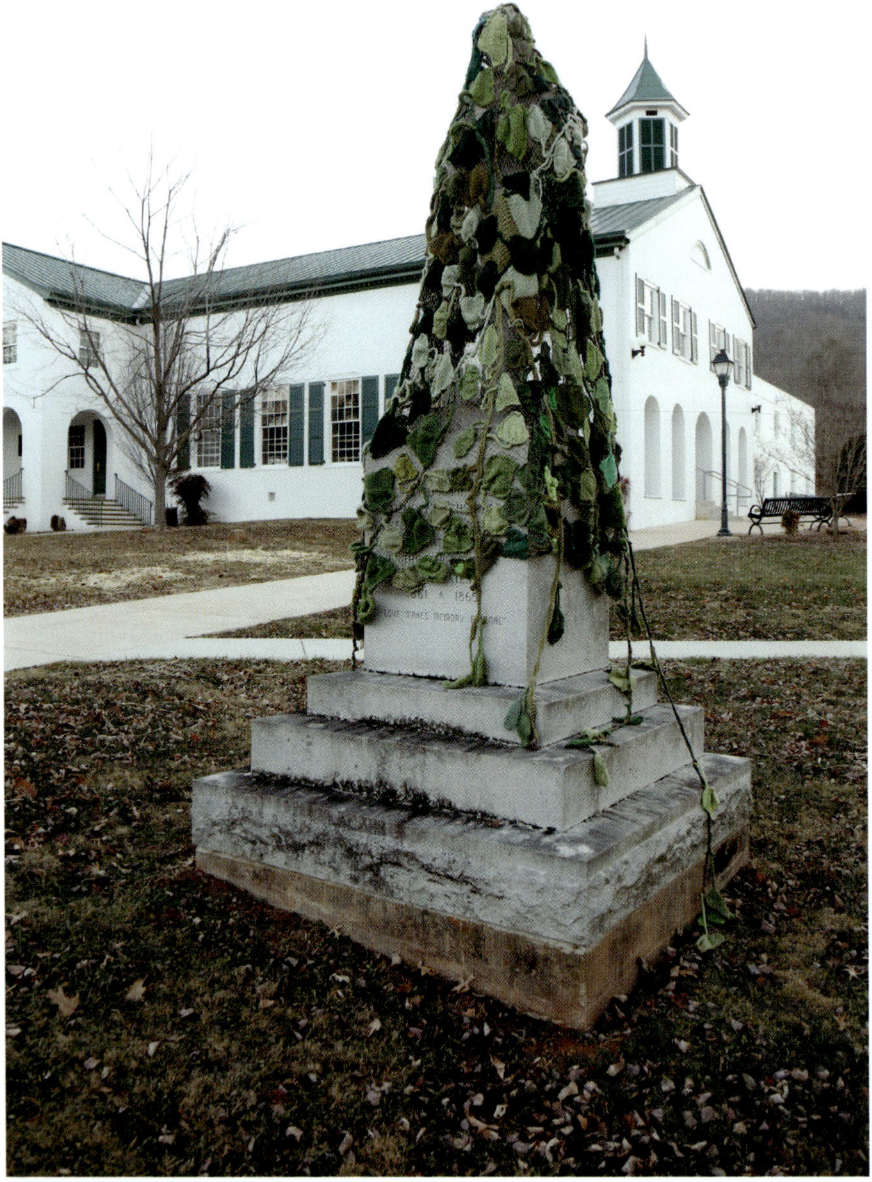

DC. While the purpose of the hat project was to create a public display of unity, the Kudzu Project maintains a high level of secrecy to maximize the impact of the installation and to protect participants from backlash by white supremacists. The organizers sent out a call for participation containing project guidelines and instructions for knitting a simple kudzu leaf. This information was disseminated knitter-to-knitter, rather than being posted on social media. Knitters could mail their kudzu leaves and vines to a post office box and thus maintain their anonymity. The project offered a form of therapeutic expression to those who had confronted violent white supremacists on the streets of Charlottesville and those who hadn't done so, but still felt violated. Participants stitched their trauma into three-lobed leaves in every shade of green. As packages arrived at the post office, organizers marveled at the mysterious networks the project had traversed—as circuitous, it seemed, as kudzu vines.

While more than thirty people from Virginia and the mid-Atlantic region participated in the Kudzu Project, eight volunteers assembled the installation piece by sewing leaves and vines to a fishing net. The net provided some structure for the finished piece, enabling rapid installation and removal. A crew of five people participated in the early morning installation on the statue of an anonymous Confederate soldier on the grounds of Albemarle County Courthouse on November 9, 2017. The date was selected to coincide with the trial of one of the white supremacists involved in the violent August rallies. The Kudzu Project went up quickly, but the placement wasn't right, so it was taken down and put up a second time. Vines dangled around the base of the statue, and one lone strand was hoisted over the soldier's rifle, which peeked out from the kudzu covering. With an hour or so left before dawn, the crew decided to grab coffee and biscuits at a nearby restaurant. Returning to the statue within fifteen minutes, they were aghast to find the kudzu installation gone. An

Installation at Nelson County Courthouse, Lovingston, Virginia, January 1, 2018. Photo: Tom Cogill

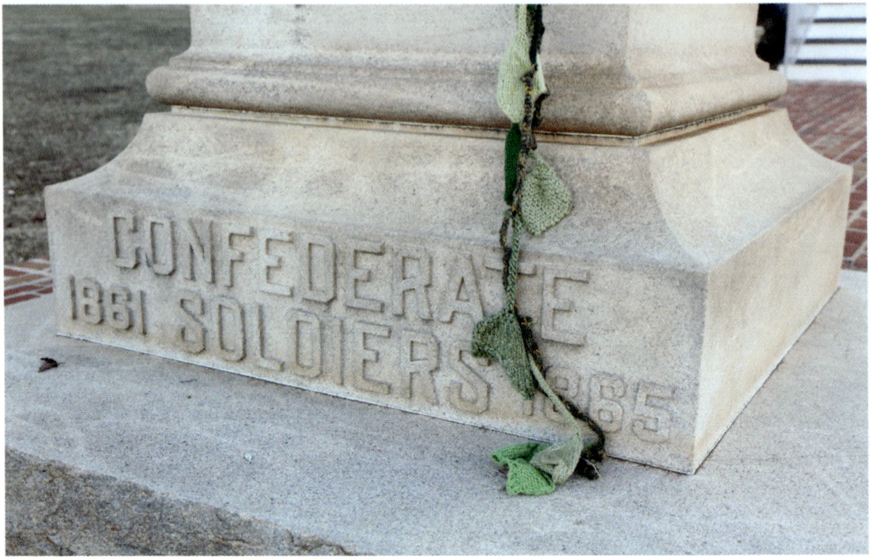

Installation at Amherst County Courthouse, Amherst, Virginia, January 1, 2018. Photo: Tom Cogill

observer surveilling the statue had removed the knitted kudzu and stuffed it into a nearby garbage bin. The crew searched up and down the street and quickly located it, then tried for the third time to launch the kudzu net over the statue, but without success.

When the crew tried to reinstall the kudzu, the observer returned to confront them and then called the police, derailing the installation. Remarkably, out of this seeming failure came a new idea for extending the life of the Kudzu Project through a series of "flash installations." These involve placing the knitted kudzu on a Confederate monument and taking photographs to document the installation before removing it. At each flash installation, a lone strand is left behind to symbolize the power and promise of small acts of resistance. Photographs of each installation are posted in a rogues' gallery on the Kudzu Project's website (www.thekudzuproject.org).

The Kudzu Project represents thousands of hours of labor by individuals who share a commitment to equity, inclusion, and social justice. The anonymity of the project makes their efforts even more remarkable. Eschewing individual recognition, participants in the Kudzu Project engaged in meaningful social action, using their talents to make a collective statement. While vinebombing Virginia's Confederate monuments may not lead to their removal, the Kudzu Project raises issues about the statues' relevance today and has given its participants a creative and public means of expressing their dissent through craft.

Margo Smith is a museum director and curator at the University of Virginia in Charlottesville, Virginia. She began knitting in 2015 and has participated in several craftivist and public art projects. Smith founded the Kudzu Project with other knitters from central Virginia following the white supremacist rallies in Charlottesville during the summer of 2017.

WORKS IN THE EXHIBITION

Allyson D. Allen
#TAKEAKNEE

2018 / Cotton, silk, satin, and denim / 42 x 41"

The movement has absolutely *nothing* to do with the military or the flag. It's about every American's right to protest peacefully. And quietly taking a knee is, to date, the most peaceful protest ever staged. Kneeling during the anthem reiterates the fact that the disproportionate number of people of color losing their lives during otherwise routine encounters with law enforcement does not equal liberty and justice for all. The first thing arresting officers yell is, "On your knees!"

Allyson D. Allen is an artist, author, instructor, and curator. She creates quilted textiles, dolls, and handmade books. Her work has been exhibited worldwide.

CONNECT

kuumba421.wix.com/quilts421

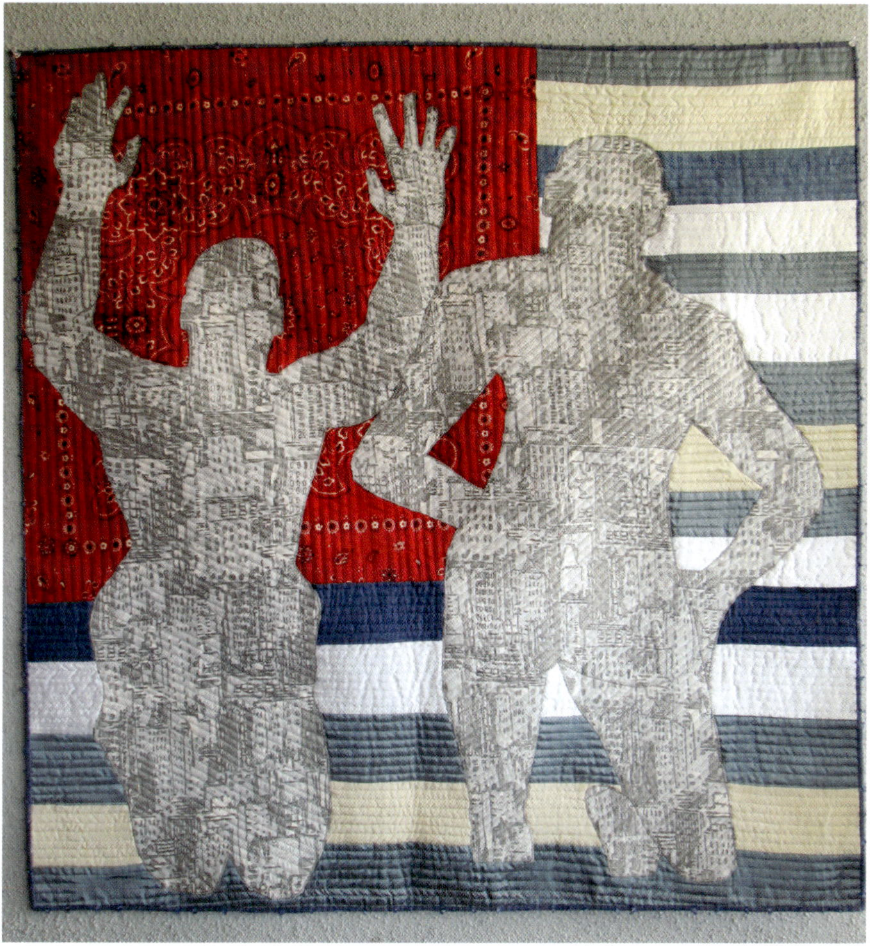

Ellis Angel
Don't Mourn, Organize

2018 / Mixed media: found Women's March posters, thread, stretcher bars / 32 x 32"

Don't Mourn, Organize is a collection of protest posters from the Women's March on NYC, January 21, 2018, that have been shredded, reassembled, and woven back together. The weaving is at once a way to bring many voices together into one, as well as a documentation of the movement. Some words can be made out, while other signs become part of the larger voice within the weaving, creating a kind of visual *E pluribus unum*. Using an art form that has historically belonged to women, this work seeks to embrace the democratic nature of raising many voices in a unified call to action—to organize.

Ellis Angel is an emerging activist artist. With a concentration in mixed media, more specifically paper weaving, Ellis seeks to reduce text and meanings to their basic parts in order to provide the viewer with a different reading of the theme. Using various texts, Ellis provides a commentary or subtle protest through the subversive nature of destroying something of value or juxtaposing texts together. Ellis has a love of the written word, having received a Masters in English with a concentration in Cultural Studies, which culmanated with a thesis on Walt Whitman's personal and political Calamus poems. Like Whitman, Ellis sees the personal as political and political as personal, and seeks to bring awareness and rememberance of current events through the art of weaving.

Don't Mourn, Organize has been shown at the Febuary 2018 Salon Greenpoint Gallery in Brooklyn, New York, as well as Beyond #MeToo 2019 at Monmouth University in West Long Branch, NJ.

CONNECT

www.ellisangel.com
Instagram: @ellis_angel1

I VOTE EQUALITY
I VOTE DIVERSITY
I VOTE HUMANITY
I VOTE RESISTANCE
VICELAND
DON'T MOURN
ORGANIZE
#Not my presiden

Christy Bailey
Cleaning America

2018 / Swiffer Sweeper, terry cloth, thread, mop gripper / 50 x 10″

MADE IN THE USA. HAND-QUILTED CLEANING ACTION. AMERICAN TOUGH. AMERICAN CLEAN.

The flag is a beautiful symbol filled with power and presence. The Stars and Stripes have also become a mass-produced symbol covering everything from can coolers, napkins, and plates, to socks, bandannas, and shoes. There is an imbalance between revering the flag and then wiping one's sweaty brow with a red, white, and blue handkerchief. *Cleaning America* came about from imagining a series of cleaning products with this patriotic symbol. How does it change the meaning of this object and its potential for activation? I am interested in how a symbol can represent power and purity, but also with dirt in its history.

My work is concerned with interpreting and remixing familiar objects, symbols, and rituals. I chose the Swiffer Sweeper as a tool that is reflective of our contemporary society and feminized the symbol of the flag within the realm of "women's work" by drawing comparisons between repetitive and meticulous domestic duties from cleaning to sewing. I look to women working with their hands to produce something of necessity and beauty, reflective of the time, and art as a meaningful and effective tool for social change.

Christy Bailey is a visual artist, educator, and musician living in Portland, Oregon. Her trans-disciplinary work creates poetry out of common things, repurposing and repositioning the everyday in an examination of the psychology of space and the presence of everyday objects.

Bailey holds an MFA in visual studies from the Pacific Northwest College of Art and received the MFA thesis award. She received her BFA from the former College of Santa Fe. Bailey exhibits locally and nationally, and has recently completed residencies at Caldera and the Hambidge Center for the Arts. Her critical work outside the studio is teaching art and music to youth.

CONNECT

christy-bailey.squarespace.com

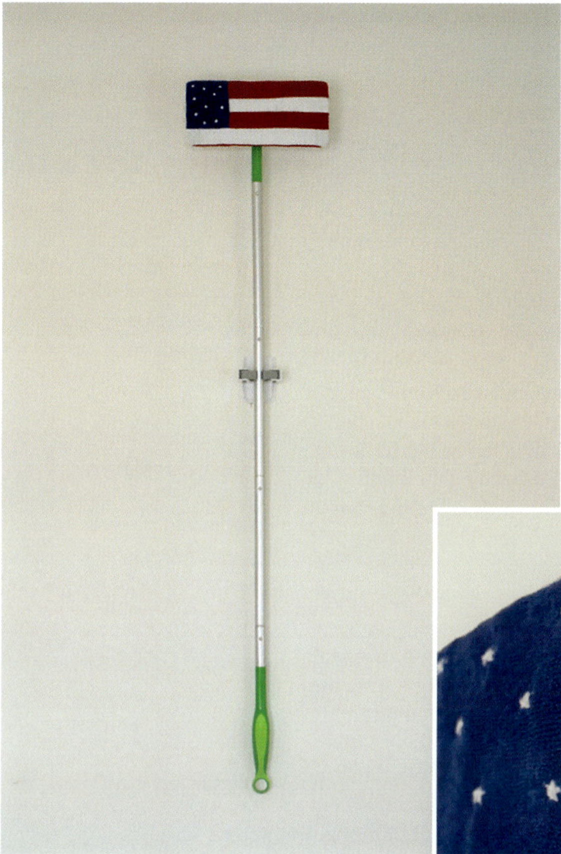

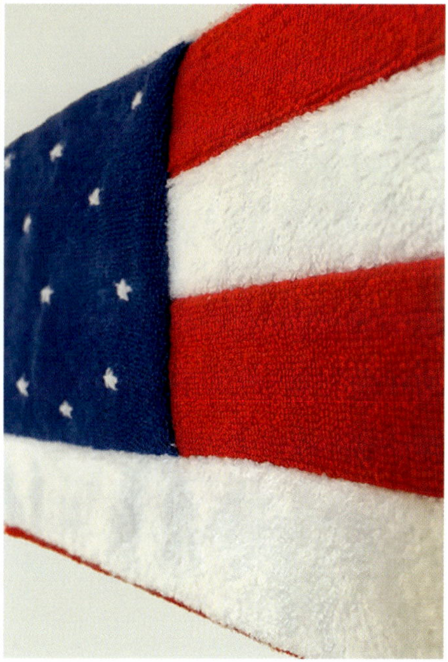

Deb J. Berkebile
Still Dreaming of Equality III

2017 / Hand-dyed cotton fabrics with screenprinting and painting with thickened dyes / 35 x 48″

My inspiration for this piece came from Rosa Parks and Martin Luther King, Jr. Their acts of nonviolent civil disobedience made them heroes, not only within the civil rights movement in America, but also for peaceful people all across the world. Most people have learned about some aspect of the civil rights movement, no matter their age. We are affected by the actions of those brave individuals, and the outcome of the movement as a whole, in our everyday lives. Due to recent current events in our country, I have become more proactive in politics: reading up on issues affecting our nation and studying how we came to be here, in this moment. I've asked myself how I can use my privilege to help others who are marginalized. How we can keep the fabric of our democracy from being tattered and torn apart in this current turmoil. Rosa Parks became a ray of light in a dark time. The dream lived on with Martin Luther King, Jr., Jane Pittman, John Lewis, Roy Wilkins, Whitney M. Young, Jr., and many more. We still have work to do, no matter our race, color, religion, or creed. Let's not be discouraged. Let's rise up and fight to keep our democracy alive and well. Let Freedom Ring! Rise Up and Vote!

Deb J. Berkebile is an artist with extensive background in textiles and quilt making. Recently, she has been exploring surface design and multimedia in her artwork. She is a naturalist and environmentalist at heart. Her current body of work explores satellite imagery and creating false-color artistic depictions of remote-sensed satellite images (geographic information systems). The vivid colors and their outstanding variations are what first drew her to these representations. She is interested in political activism, which inspired a series of works about civil rights. Her work has been displayed at the Space for Art exhibit at NASA Space Center in Houston, Texas, and at the United States Military Academy at West Point in New York. Her award-winning quilt, *Rafiki—the Great Mystic*, was one of the finalists selected by Disney Theatrical Group to be exhibited at Minskoff Theatre in New York City in 2017.

CONNECT

mountaintrailquilttreasure.blogspot.com
https://www.facebook.com/DebBerkebile

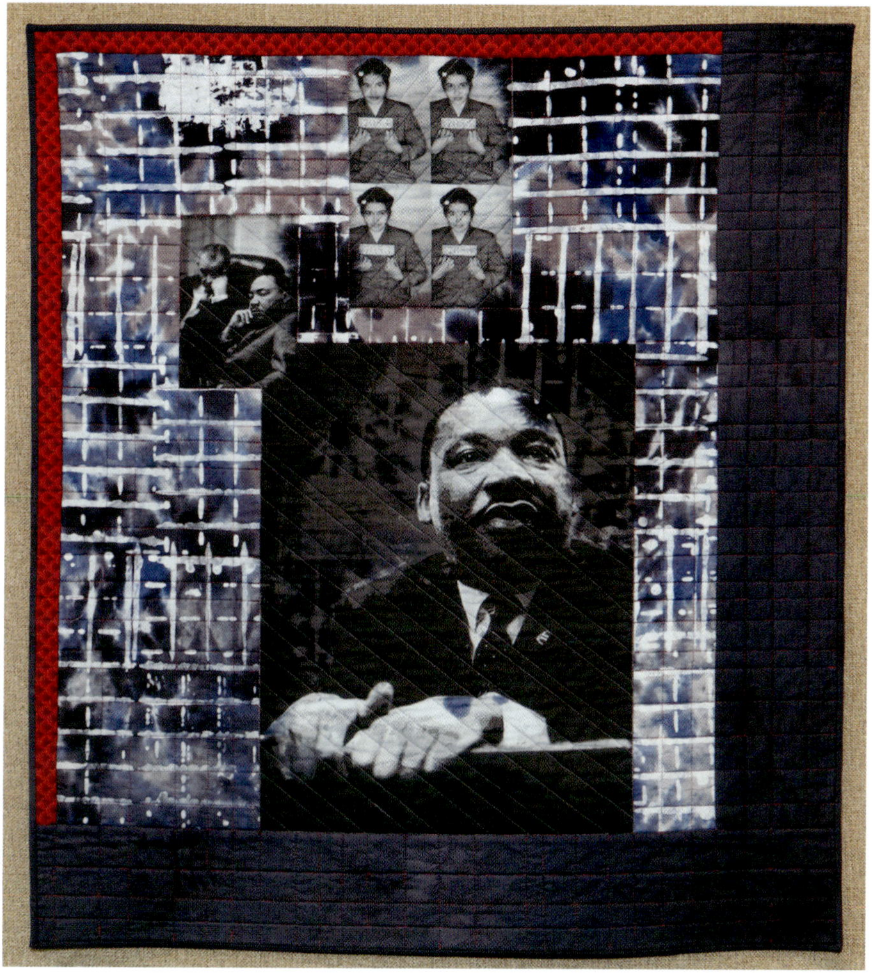

Eva Camacho-Sanchez
Enough

2018 / Merino wool, silk, cotton thread / 24 x 40″

What will it take? How many more lives? It seems like no amount of killing is enough for Congress to take action on guns. It seems that each mass shooting in America makes us more desensitized to the horror. This piece aims to keep us sensitive to these ongoing tragedies. How many more lives do we need to lose so our politicians are finally forced to do something, anything, to try to end the bloodshed? What is enough? Killing twenty six- and seven-year-olds in an elementary school is not enough. More than five hundred injured and almost sixty killed at an outdoor concert in Las Vegas, and fifty killed at a night club in Orlando is also not enough. When is enough enough?

Eva Camacho-Sanchez is a fiber artist born and raised in Andalusia, Spain, now living in Massachusetts. Her work fuses the ancient art form of felt making with modern techniques to create new and elegant styles. She uses natural and biodegradable materials with an emphasis on low-impact environmental and creative processes. Camacho-Sanchez usually starts by hand dyeing the wool fibers (with natural dyes she creates from plant matter), which are then felted together with fine silk. To create patterns on the silk, she uses techniques such as free-motion embroidery, hand stitching, beading, and printing. Although she is devoted to felt, Eva is equally intrigued by other media, fibers, and fabrics.

CONNECT

www.evacamacho.com
Instagram:
@evacamacho_studio
https://www.facebook.com/Eva.Camacho.Sanchez

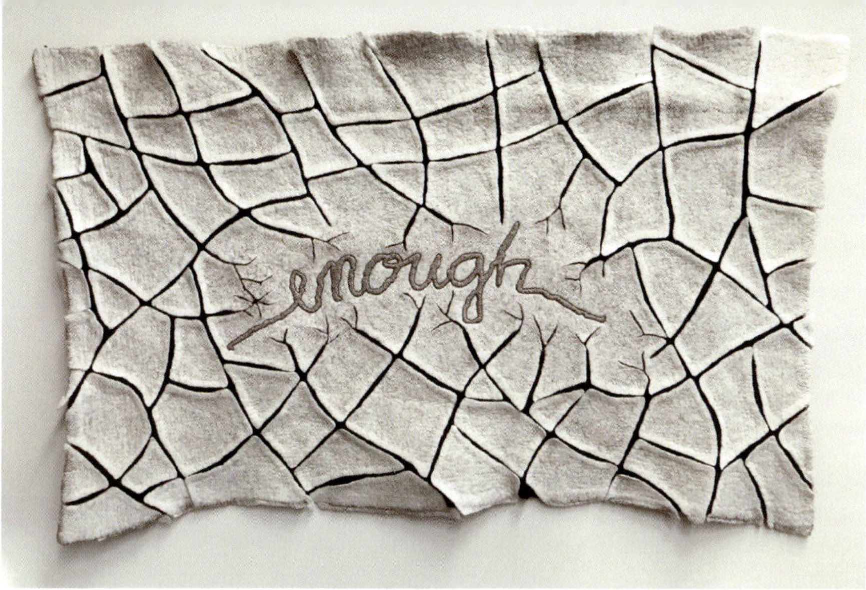
enough

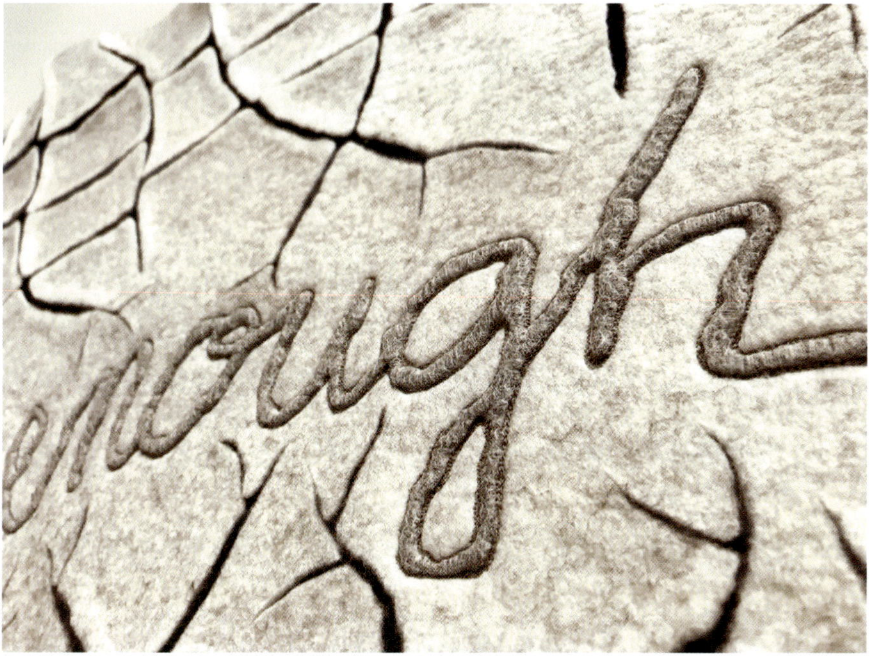

Margaret A. Cherre
Will It Ever End

2018 / Rayon chenille yarn / Approximately 10" wide x 72" circumference

I used colors deliberately in this handwoven piece: white represents the people in power, generally white men, and their use of power to remain in control of resources; black represents people without power, generally people of color, striving for equality and justice; red represents the blood that is shed in those struggles; purple represents women, especially those actively seeking equality; and gold represents voting rights.

After weaving, I joined the fabric in a never-ending mobius strip, since many of the struggles faced by Frederick Douglass and Susan B. Anthony continue today. Racism and sexism are unfortunately still major influences in our lives: bloodshed continues, especially for black men, and through gerrymandering and lack of voting rights for felons and undocumented people, disenfranchisement remains a problem for many.

With Washington's anti-immigration laws and actions, lack of respect for women's lives, work, and bodies, disdain for people of color, and continued expansion of the wealth of the few at the expense of the rest, I believe Douglass and Anthony would be both saddened and angered at the state of the country. We need to continue the groundswell of local activism that began after the 2016 election.

Margaret A. Cherre is a professional handweaver and a Master Artisan in weaving with the Roycrofters-At-Large Association. She shows and sells her work at a limited number of juried fine art and craft shows in western New York State, as well as at the Copper Shop on the Roycroft campus.

Margaret's interest in working with fiber began as a child, weaving potholders on a little metal loom. Having spent years sewing, knitting, and creating for herself and her family, Margaret plunged into the world of weaving professionally after her retirement as a not-for-profit administrator. Her work is known for her use of color, fine threads, and complex weave patterns. Predominantly self-taught, she primarily weaves on two vintage floor looms that she carefully restored to working order.

CONNECT

www.handwovenscarves.com
www.secondwindjewelry.com/jewelry-weaving-blog

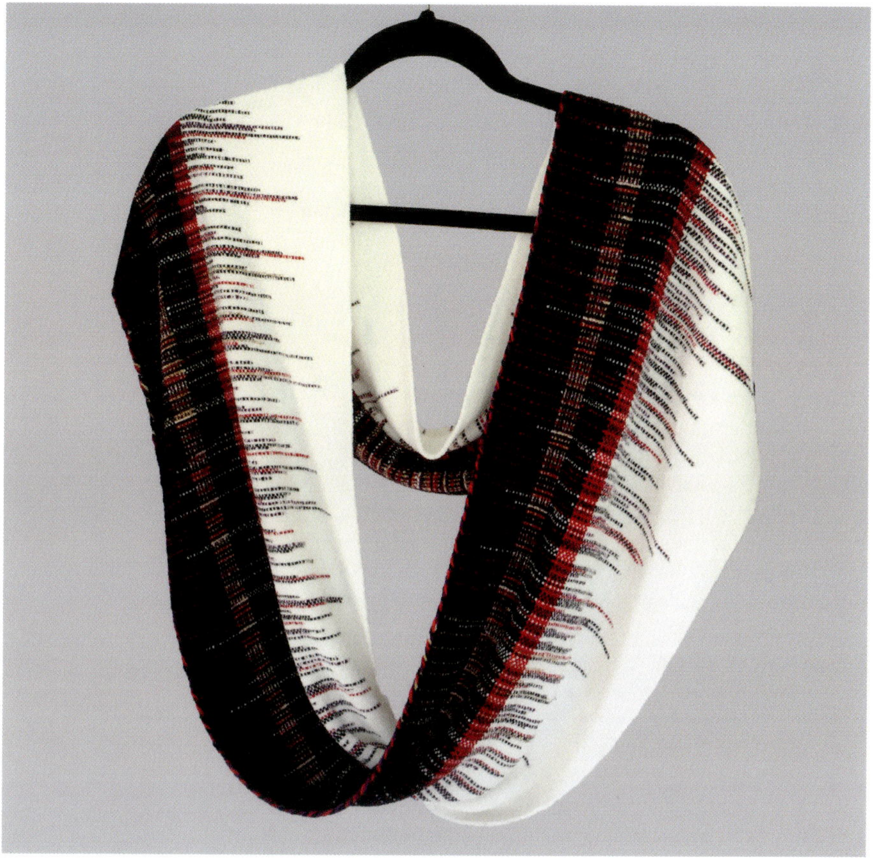

Anna J. Clutterbuck-Cook
Persistent Stitches I

2018 / Cotton print fabric, cotton batting, cotton thread, cotton embroidery floss, metal bottle cap discs, epoxy stickers, paper, ink, pencil, and glue / 42 x 12 x 0.25"

During the months leading up to the 2016 presidential election, Anna began to cross-stitch the Hillary Clinton campaign logo using the colors of the US women's suffrage campaign: purple, white, and gold. Her hope was to commemorate, through needlework, the historic moment when the United States elected its first woman president. On election night, she set the piece aside unfinished. *Persistent Stitches I* incorporates this incomplete work, abandoned in a moment of grief and fear, as the second of five quilted windowpanes looking out over past actions and future possibilities. Through each window grow tenacious vines, finding root in the cracks and crevices of our past, present, and future. The vines flower with images and words collected from friends and family, each representing ways people have sustained themselves, their communities, and their world during this time of brokenness. This new growth represents our commitment to work toward a more equitable and sustainable future as the unfinished cross-stitch is both overtaken by and incorporated into a dense, living tangle of collective social justice labor.

Anna J. Clutterbuck-Cook grew up in a family of artists and crafters, learning to crochet, cross-stitch, embroider, knit, sew, and weave as a child. Primarily a knitter in adolescence and young adulthood, she drifted away from handcrafts during graduate school. The gift of a quilting class at a local craft store in 2015 renewed her interest in fiber arts. Quilting and embroidery became a new opportunity to play with color, design, and handwork. In January 2018, she launched Persistent Stitches (persistentstitches.org), an all-volunteer, grassroots collective that raises money, through crafting, for organizations doing social justice work and resisting the Republican agenda. This is her first juried art show. When not stitching, Anna serves as a reference librarian at the Massachusetts Historical Society, is a reader and writer of romance, and pursues her scholarly interest in the history of American Protestant engagement with new understandings of gender, sex, sexuality, and race. She lives with her wife and two cats in Roslindale, Massachusetts.

CONNECT

thefeministlibrarian.com
Twitter: @feministlib

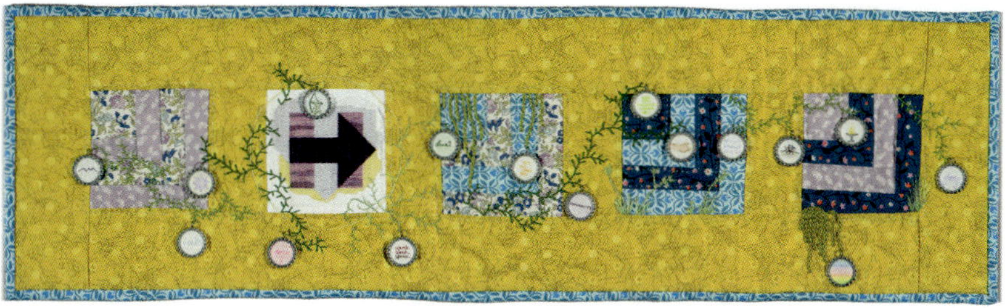

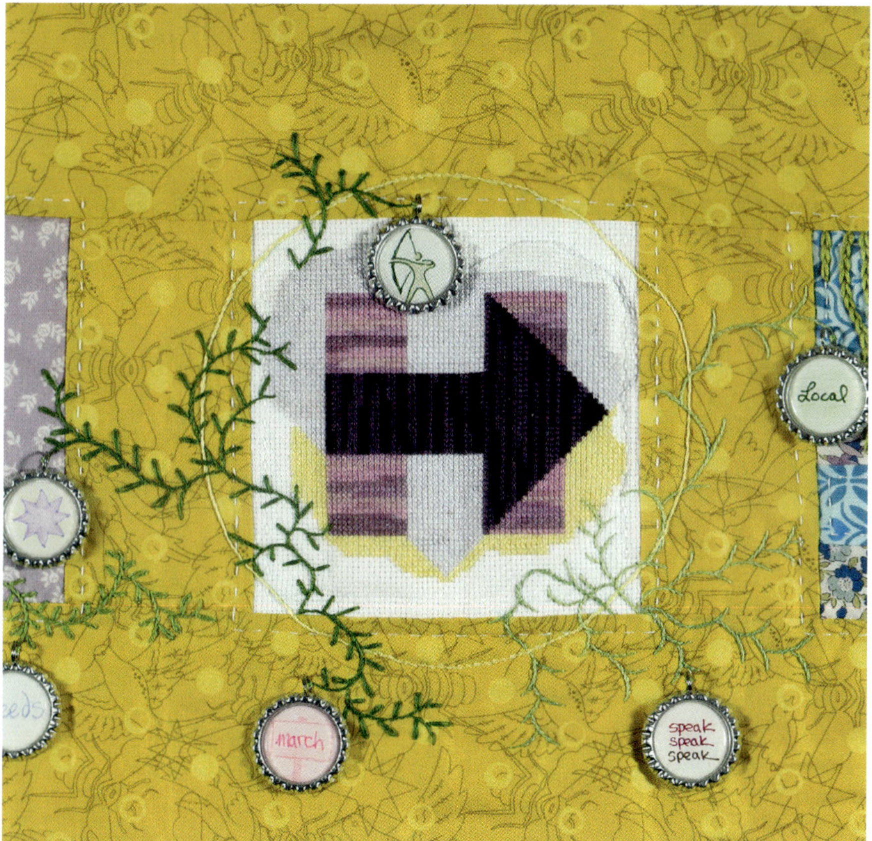
Local
march
speak
speak
speak

Sonja Dahl
Whitework: Race Traitor

2018 / Jacquard woven cotton thread / 28.25 x 26.5"

Sonja Dahl's ongoing series of projects under the conceptual banner of *Whitework* uses metaphors and techniques drawn from historic white-on-white textiles to probe the contemporary cultural shift in which the benefits of white identity are simultaneously contested and championed on the public stage. This body of work explores how cloth might function as a call to action for dedicated and focused white work in contemporary society, requiring those of us who benefit from systemic and cultural whiteness to awaken from historical amnesia and take responsibility for our embeddedness in systems of oppression.

Taking the shape of a banner, *Race Traitor* makes a nod to the material history of past and present social movements. This piece is about entanglement and resistance, and the productively treasonous activities of those who reject the terms of their membership in dominant white culture. Recalling the hundreds of entangled threads faced when dressing the loom, this weaving might serve as an apt reminder that embedded in the material DNA of our social fabric is the threads' spirit of resistance to order. *Whitework* grows from such little accumulating acts of treason: the rise and fall of needle and thread piercing cloth, rearranging the weave structure, one stitch at a time.

Sonja Dahl is an artist, writer, and research associate in the Department of Art at the University of Oregon, Eugene. She draws from a textiles background in her artwork, and in her scholarship delves into the cultural, economic, historic, and metaphoric aspects of how textiles and textile processes live within and reflect the values of human societies. Her recent projects focus on the colonial history and contemporary trending of indigo dye in the United States, as well as an ongoing project titled *Whitework*, which uses historic white-on-white textiles as an entry point to discuss the cultural constructs of whiteness. Sonja received her MFA from Cranbrook Academy of Art (2012), her BFA from the University of Oregon (2010), and her BA from California Lutheran University (2001). Her artwork has been exhibited nationally and internationally, and her writing is published in both peer-reviewed journals, and print-based and online arts publications.

CONNECT

www.sonjakdahl.com
Instagram: @sonjakdahl
https://www.facebook.com/sonja.dahl.39?ref=br_rs

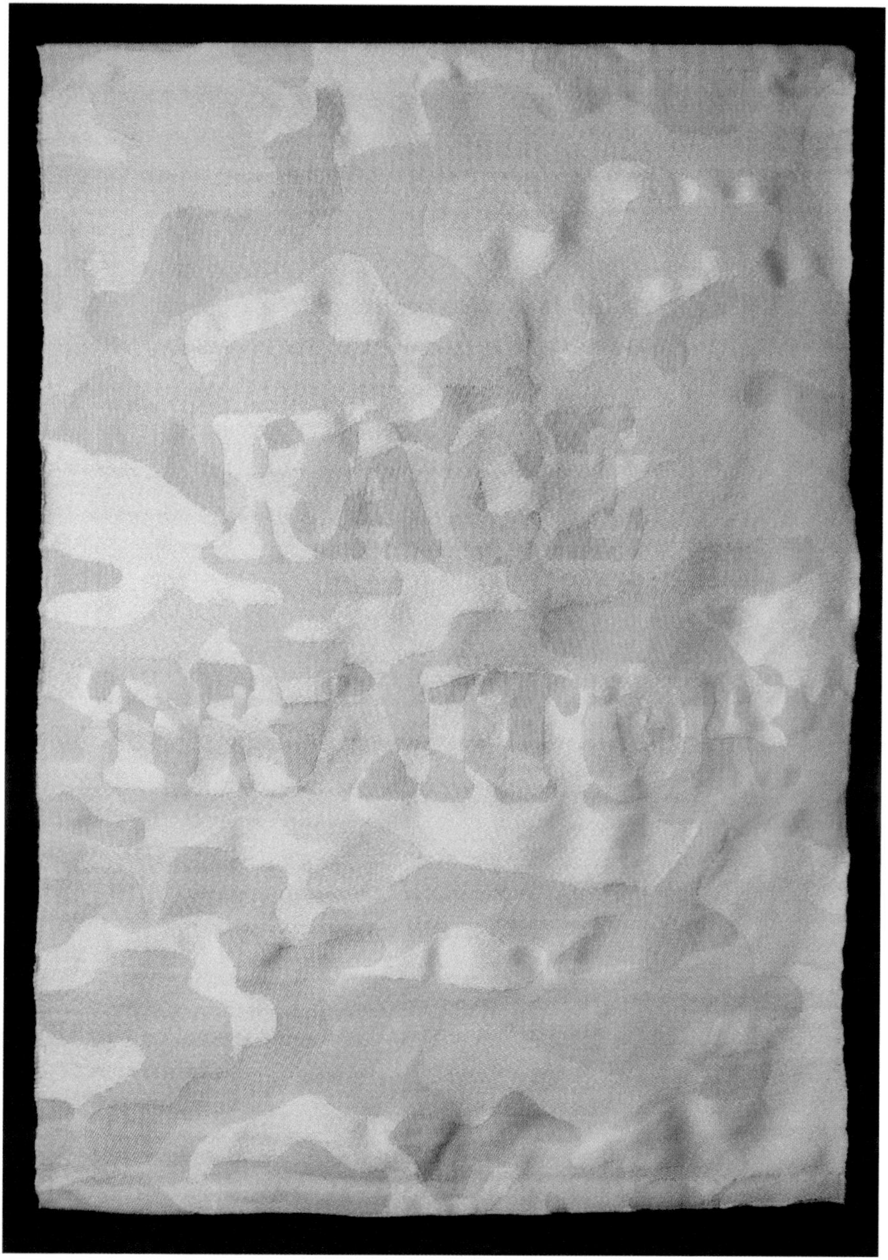

Alison Flaherty / Carin Horowitz / Hinda Mandell / Penny Schmuecker / Elizabeth Sovern

Cross-Stitch and Yarn Marker Commemorating the First Frederick Douglass Family House in Rochester, New York

2017 / Yarn, sequins, thread, canvas mesh, pom-poms / 36 x 9"

Sometimes the domestic tools of yarn and thread can be a colorful Band-Aid for drawing attention to historic erasure and attempting to correct it. An address in downtown Rochester, New York, located at 297 Alexander Street, is a parking lot, but historically it was the site of the first house inhabited by Anna and Frederick Douglass in 1848 when they moved to Rochester with their children. The Douglass family welcomed freedom seekers into their home there, a stop on the Underground Railroad. This remarkable piece of history has fallen victim to the 1954 blades of bulldozers and urban renewal. In an attempt to commemorate the historic provenance of this spot, before an official marker was erected there in the fall of 2018, handicraft proved a useful tool to indicate to passersby the historic nature of this address. Through social media, Hinda Mandell released a call for knit and crochet panels to be sent to Rochester, forming a textile piece that Hinda then wrapped around a tree by the parking lot.
A cross-stitch by the Rochester artist Alison Flaherty, in the shape of a New York State historic marker, further commemorated the spot.

Alison Flaherty, originally of Dansville, New York, who now resides in Rochester, NY, works with traditional cross-stitch methods to create contemporary pieces reflecting today's culture and attitudes. Carin Horowitz (New York) is a social worker in the disabilities field and a knitter of eight years. Hinda Mandell (New York) is an associate professor in the School of Communication at RIT. Elizabeth Sovern (New York) is founder of craftivist.net. Penny Schmuecker (Nebraska) started knitting three years ago and is driven by the idea of crafters coming together to raise consciousness in a way that not only is nonviolent, but also makes the world a more beautiful place.

CONNECT

craftivist.net / thenerdyoctopus.com / omghinda.com
Twitter: @crochetactivism
https://www.facebook.com/nerdyoctopus/
https://www.facebook.com/CraftivistUSA/

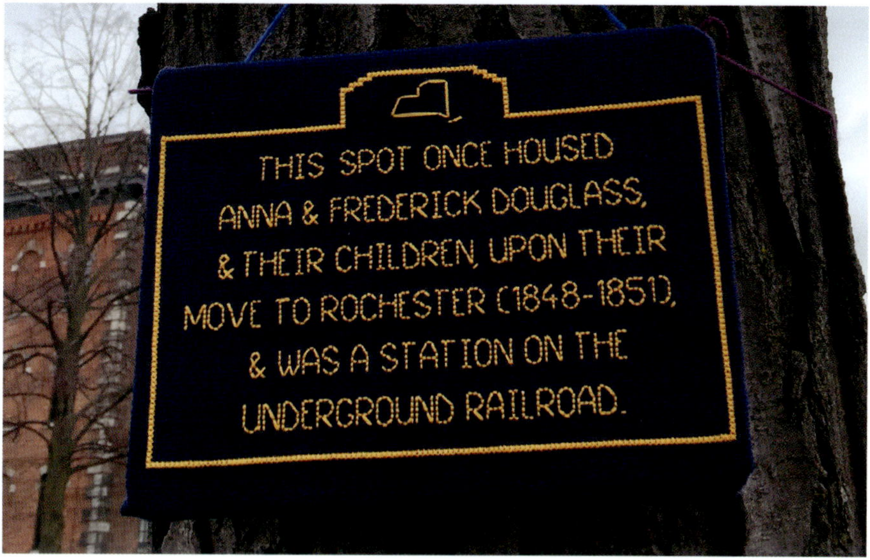
THIS SPOT ONCE HOUSED
ANNA & FREDERICK DOUGLASS,
& THEIR CHILDREN, UPON THEIR
MOVE TO ROCHESTER (1848-1851),
& WAS A STATION ON THE
UNDERGROUND RAILROAD.

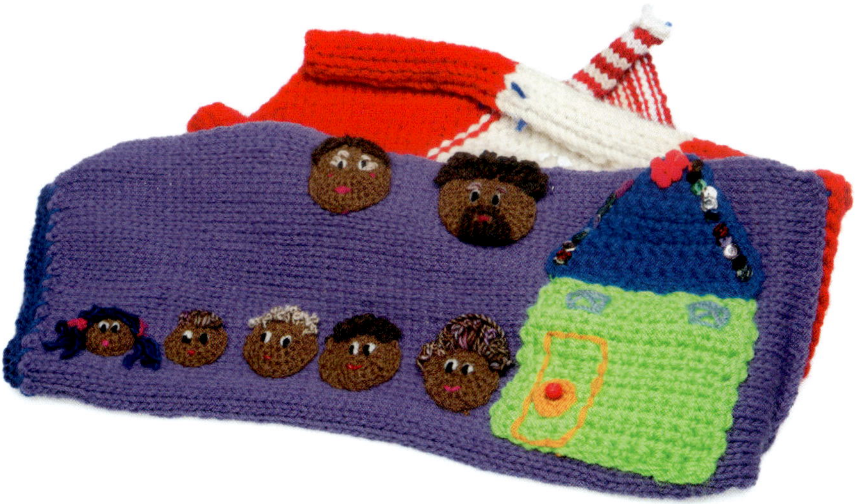

Katrina L. Herron Gendreau
Female Inheritance

2018 / Linen with silk embroidery thread / 11 x 17″

Girlhood samplers are often viewed as implements of obsequious isolation for women throughout history. They also attest to skilled artistry and remain a lasting and rare record of women's experiences to fill the void of written history from such marginalized populations. Herron Gendreau became steeped in the art form while working with historical textile collections in graduate school and found it a fertile medium for addressing complex ideas about the expected versus real ideals and nature ascribed to womanhood from past to present.

The motifs here are drawn from the 1774 sampler of Elizabeth Derby in Salem, Massachusetts. Derby became a rare divorcée in 1806 after a widely publicized and bitter trial. Her story is an especially unusual one of upheaval and a bittersweet independence following a conventional upbringing that the now somewhat ironic symbol of her sampler attests to.

Female Inheritance is a reflection upon the artistry of the medium, as well as the expectations of womanhood within early and modern American society. In embracing and subverting the medium, the work seeks to capture fundamental changes occurring within our society in regard to gender and identity politics.

Katrina Herron Gendreau is a textile artist and educator in Detroit, Michigan. She double majored in art and art history at Hope College and earned a Master of Liberal Arts within the museum studies program at Harvard University Extension School.

CONNECT

www.khgarts.com
Instagram: @khgarts

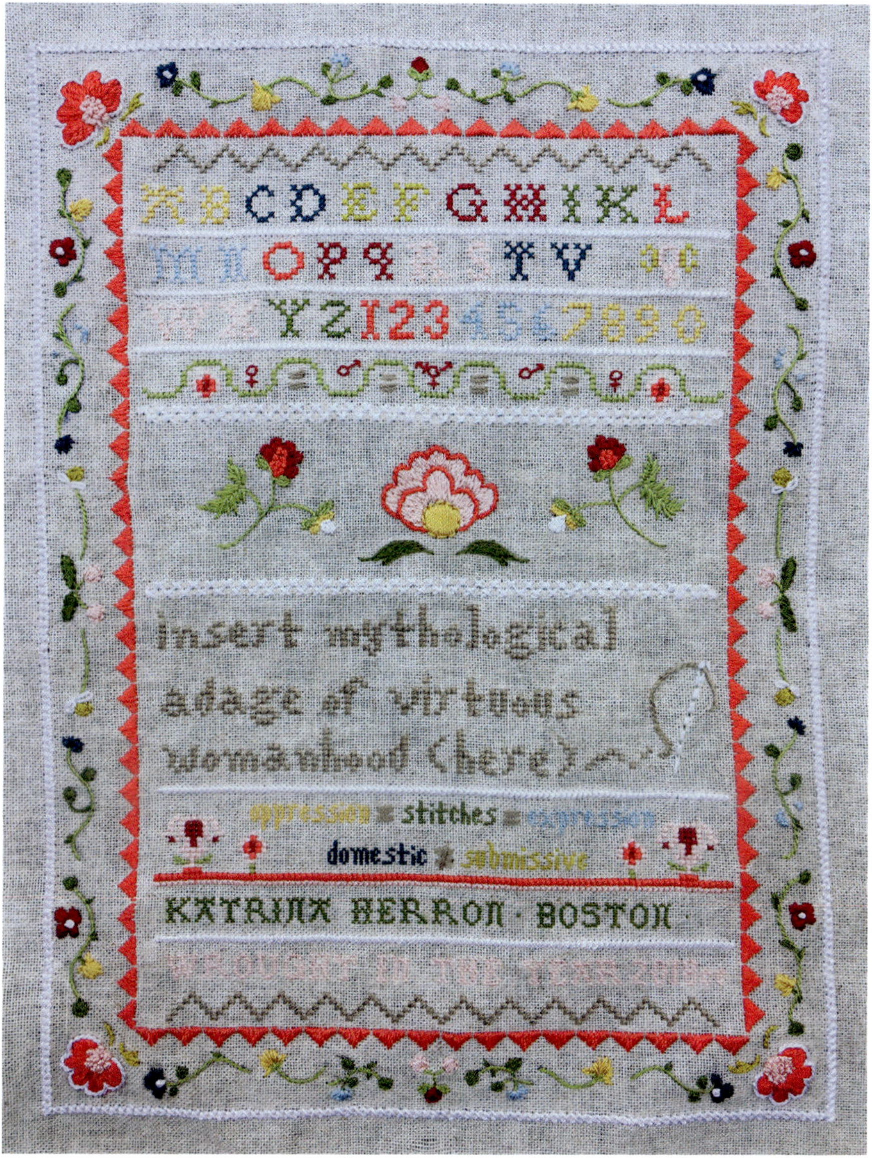
insert mythological
adage of virtuous
womanhood (here)
oppression stitches expression
domestic submissive
KATRINA HERRON · BOSTON

Suzanne Hesh
Color, Gender, Power, Order

2016 / Cotton fabric with cotton embroidery floss, found material / 15 x 18"

Color, Gender, Power, Order is a visual expression of a four-word description of the elements of the systems of Western society in general and the United States specifically. With which element do you most closely identify? Which element is the basis of your personal power? What is the relationship of each element in your personal and social life?

The use of traditional textile media and processes is often associated with "women's work" and feminine pursuits. Here, and increasingly in the art world, they intentionally defy the life-and-death struggle between the four elements as manifested within and between people and social and political institutions.

Suzanne Hesh is a textile artist living in the Sonora Desert in Tucson, Arizona. She has a Bachelor of Fine Art and Master of Arts from the University of Arizona. Prior to committing to a life of full-time creativity, she taught art in the public schools for nearly three decades. Through the intimate medium of textile, her art expresses big ideas: psychological, social, political, or spiritual themes that have personal meaning and universal application. Hesh uses events, public or private, which expose or present alternatives to the relationship of people to each other or to the world. Her work calls for a shift in understanding and for a new response to the deep and complex nature of human experience.

Hesh is a textile artist because it's the medium that has been closest to her for all of her life. She regards the use of textiles as a positive challenge to create meaningful art from a material that is ancient, mundane, benign, complex, and accessible. Hesh has exhibited her work nationally since 1995.

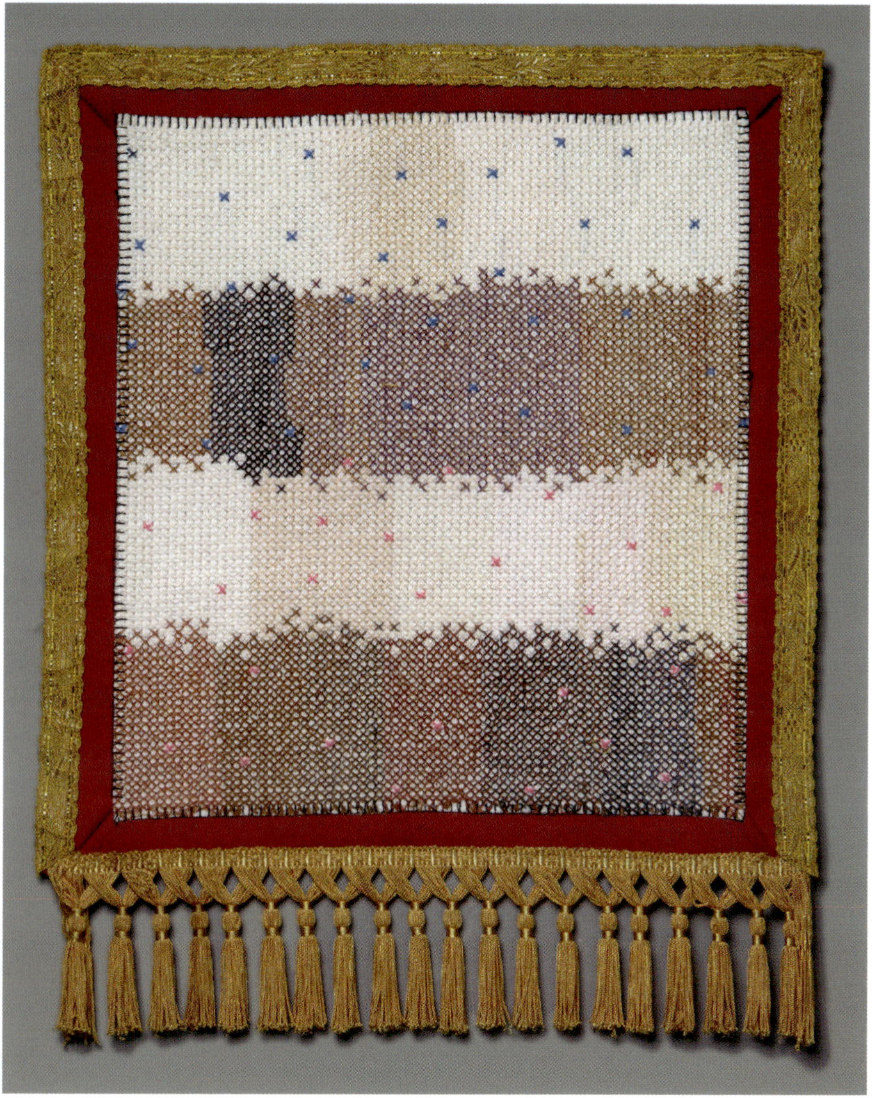

Chawne M. Kimber
Cotton Sophisticate

2015 / 100 percent cotton: US-farmed and US-woven fabrics, batting, and hand-dyed threads / 72 x 72"

"In essence, I am a sophisticated cotton picker," represents a summary quote in south Georgia native Eartha Kitt's autobiography *Alone With Me*, which has myriad (direct and indirect) meanings about labor in the textile industry, identity and difference in the US, and American cultural progress. This improvisational patchwork and kantha-style hand quilting is a direct callback to the make-do utility quilts made by the artist's great-grandmother on a former plantation in Wedowee, Alabama, at the turn of the last century. A small bit of visible mending is a love note to her.

Chawne Kimber is an award-winning textile artist who exhibits quilts and embroidery in museums, galleries, and festivals all over the United States. Through cultivation of cotton in rural Alabama, some of her ancestors (unwillingly) participated in building the United States. Inspired by quilts made by these ancestors in the late 1800s, Chawne interprets traditional patchwork forms in an improvisational style and indulges in political confrontations in quilt form.

When not manipulating cotton, Chawne is professor of mathematics at a small liberal arts college in the Northeast US.

CONNECT

cauchycomplete.wordpress.com
Instagram and Twitter: @cauchycomplete

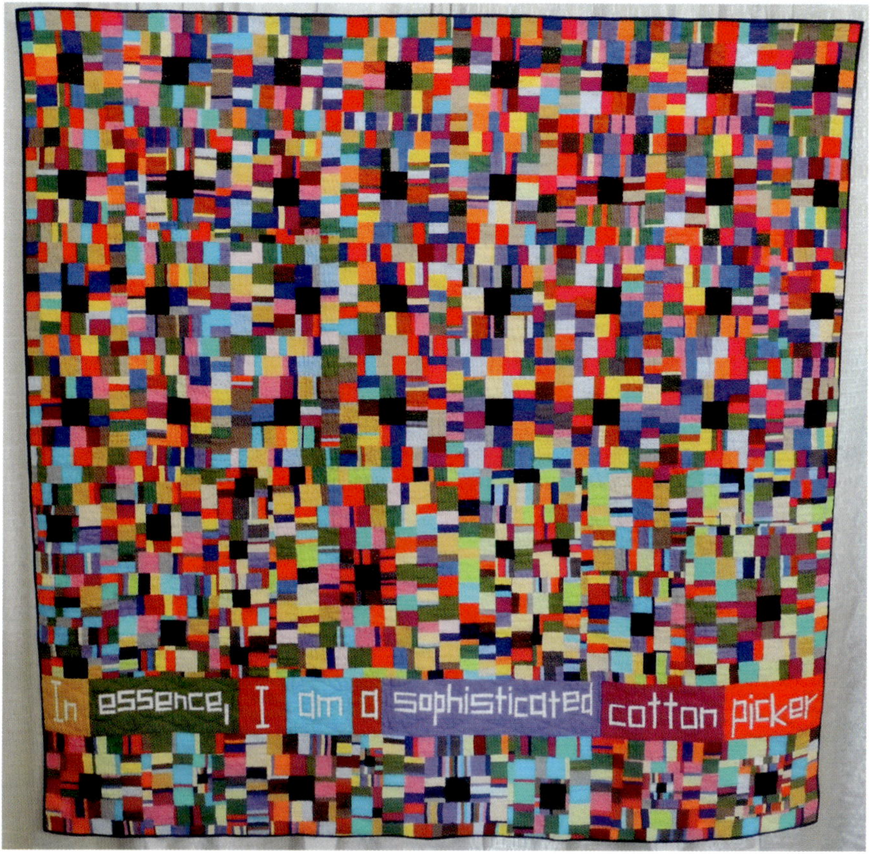
In essence, I am a sophisticated cotton picker

Jessica Lacher-Feldman

Our War Cry

2017-18 / Cotton with cotton embroidery floss / 9 x 9"

This piece was started the weekend of the first Women's Marches, January 21, 2017, as a show of solidarity and expression of pride as people came together across the world in protest and to make their voices heard. The continuous and solitary act of stitching these words, in pinks as an homage to the Pussyhat, gives sustained reflection on the power that day and as a way to remain energized in organizing, agitating, and educating, following in Susan B. Anthony's and countless others' footsteps.

Jessica Lacher-Feldman is an archivist and special collections librarian in Rochester, New York. She likens her embroidery work to "slow doodling" —drawing, and more often writing, with pencil or silver Sharpie marker on black cotton, and embellishing with cotton floss. Self-taught, she uses embroidery as a form of relaxation and meditation, as well as self-expression.

Must be
ORGANIZE
AGITATE AND
EDUCATE
our war cry!*
-SBA

June Lee
Bystander

2012-18 / Thread on resin cast / 1.5 x 8 x 2"

My work focuses on the individual in contemporary society today. I explore the neutrality and duality of the individual as a distinct unit and again as a constituent of the collective society. In particular, I shed light on the social phenomena surrounding the individual in contemporary social space, especially on negative conditions such as bystander effect, mass psychology, scapegoating, and biases. Using an East Asian element of thread, which represents human life, to form humanlike figures, my art looks at the problems of modern humanity from a third-person perspective.

June Lee was born in Seoul, South Korea, and moved to the US at age eighteen. She received her BFA at the School of the Art Institute of Chicago and an MFA in fiber at Cranbrook Academy of Art, located in Michigan. After graduating, she moved back to South Korea to work and currently teaches in Seoul. She exhibits her work in shows and participates in residency programs internationally.

CONNECT

www.junelee.kr
Instagram: @artist_junelee

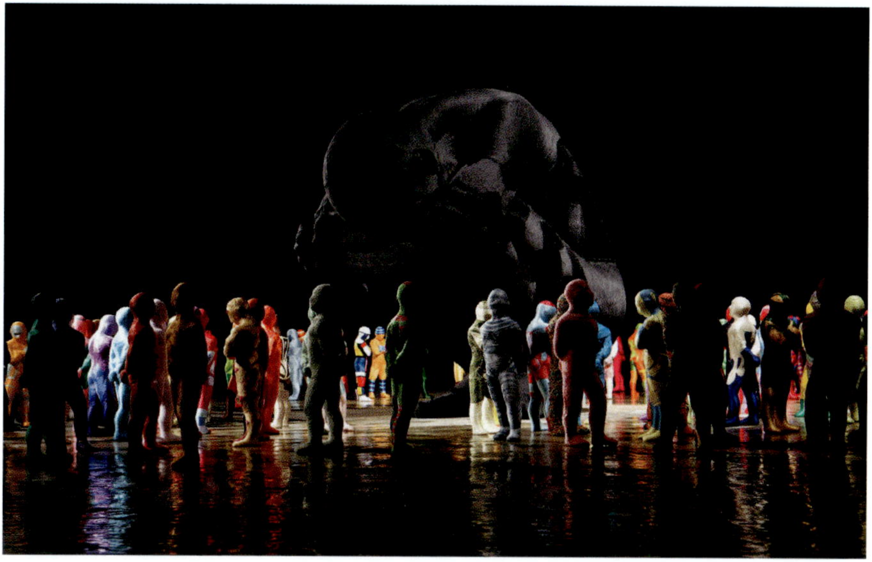

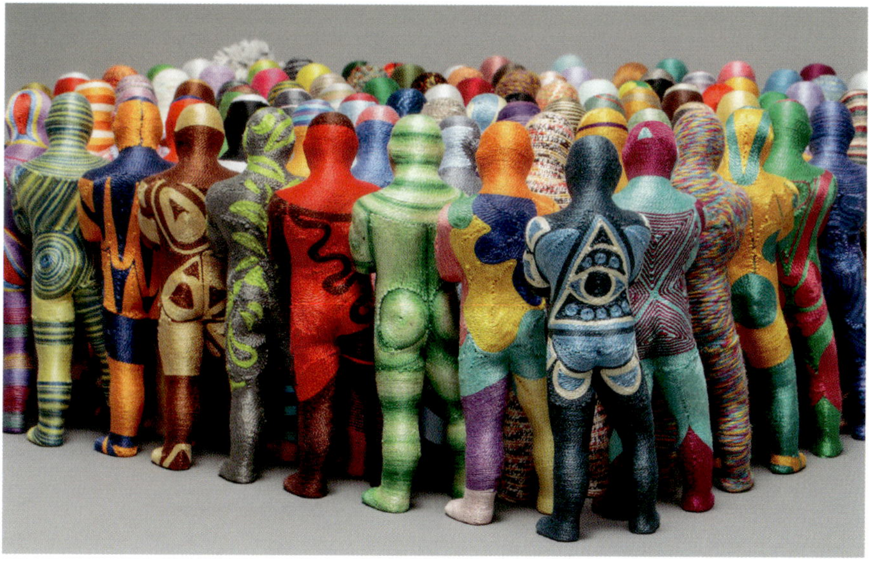

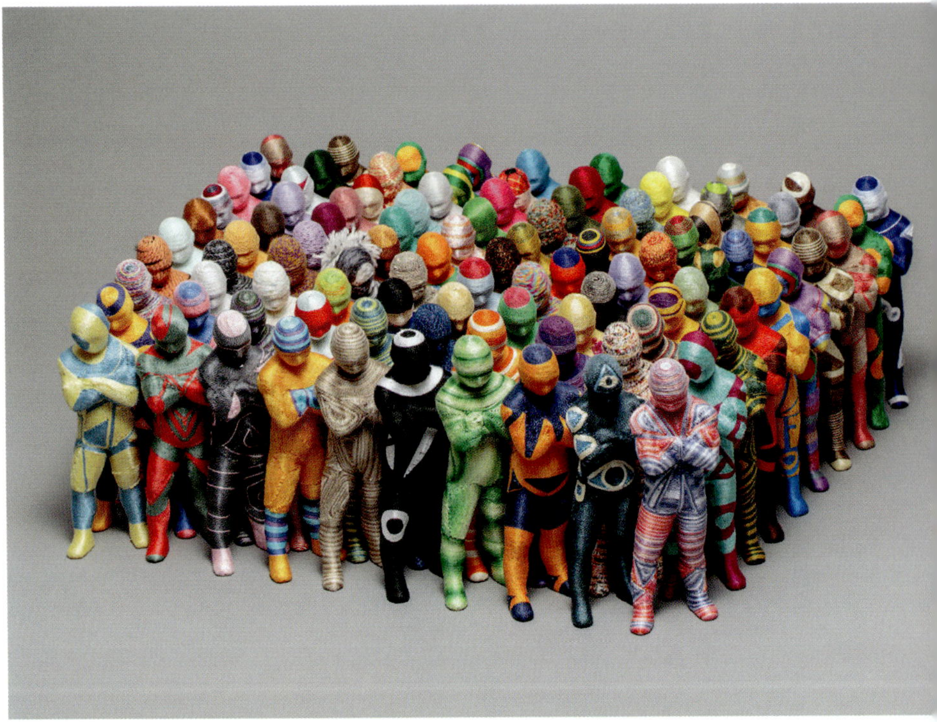

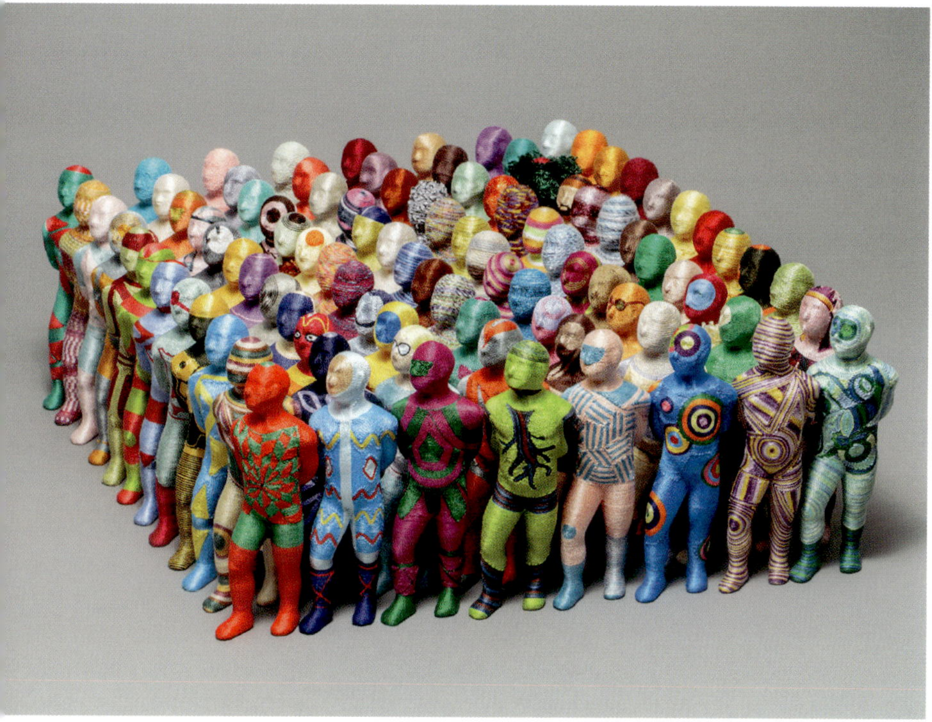

Betsy Liano
Written on My Chest

2018 / Perendale wool by Beka Simpkin's of New Zealand in color Sweet Violet / 26 x 32"

Written on My Chest has inspirational quotes from notable women that my daughters and I admire, chain stitched upon the bodice. These words of wisdom reflect our passions and inclinations, as well as articulating our response to the 2016 election. My activist daughter selected her favorite Margaret Mead quote: "Never doubt that a small group of citizens can change the world. Indeed, it is the only thing that ever has." My eldest daughter, never able to stand by silently, selected a quote by Malala Yousafzai: "When the whole world is silent, even one voice is powerful." Our family, especially my youngest, adores J. K. Rowling and the Harry Potter books; thus she selected, "Soon, we must all face the choice between what is right and what is easy." In response to the hateful behavior being fomented by the current presidential administration, I chose, "Spread love wherever you go" by Mother Theresa. I concluded the piece with Susan B. Anthony's "Failure is impossible" to give us hope for the future of democracy and our planet. This feminine sweater, designed by Mary Neal Meador, is knit with violet wool to represent the primary color of the suffragist movement. I believe systemic misogyny contributed to our current political situation. It is imperative for women to stand up and take action.

Betsy Liano is a knitting and painting instructor in Rochester, New York. She learned to knit at age five and has continued expanding her skills, including designing her own patterns. She loves to pass along knitting knowledge to others as a tribute to her mother. Betsy has been an active member of the Rochester Knitting Guild since 1997. She enjoys exploring other fiber arts, including sewing, embroidery, and felting—both wet and needle felting—which she considers painting with fibers. Betsy is also an accomplished watercolor artist. She currently serves on the board of the Pittsford Art Group. She exhibits works through local rotating exhibits and annually at Rochester Public Market Artist Row. Prints of her paintings are available at Eleventh Hour in Twelve Corners, Brighton, New York.

CONNECT

betsylianowatercolors@weebly.com

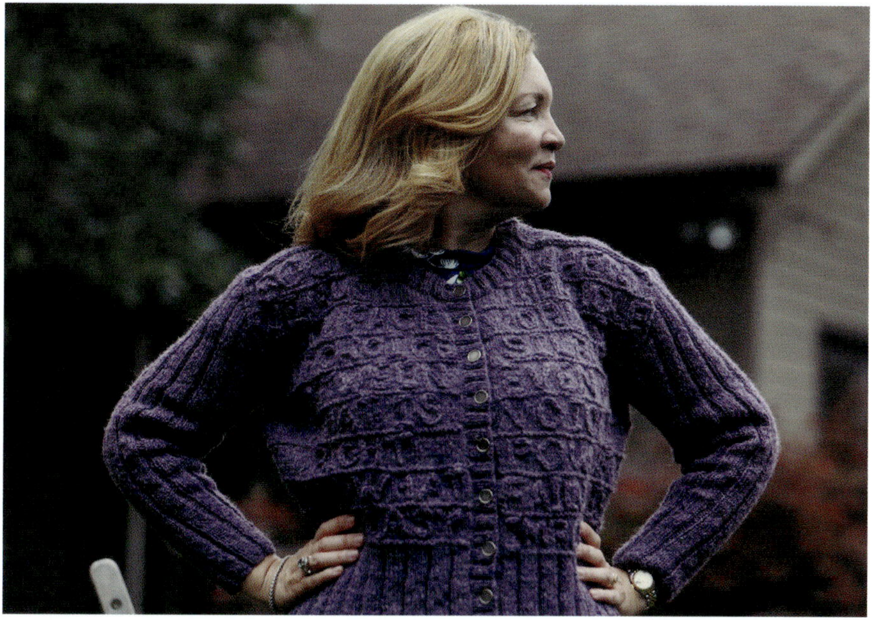

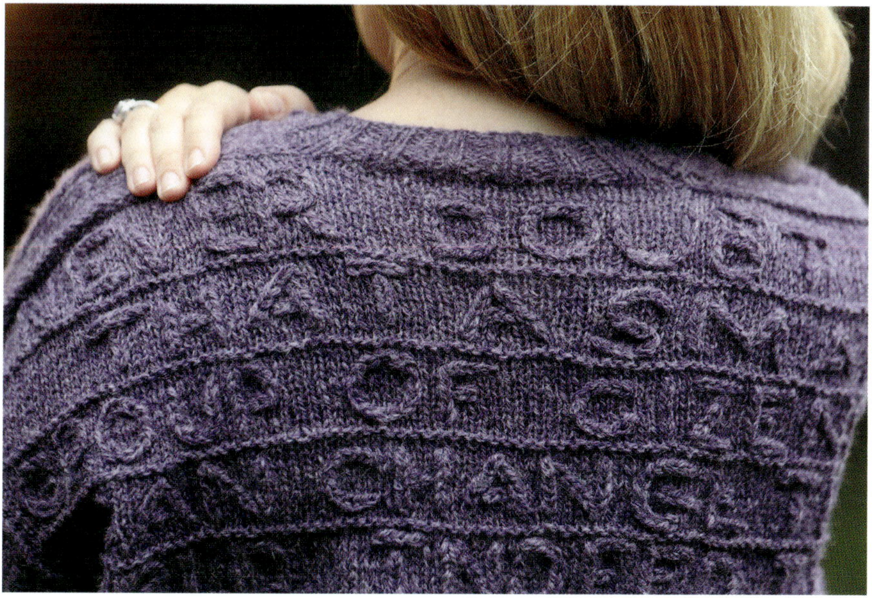

Beth Ann MacVittie
Nevertheless She Persisted

2017 / Cotton / 44 x 17"

I became passionately political after the devastating 2016 so-called election. I am a member of the Livingston County Democratic Committee, and I am becoming more informed and active with the village of Mount Morris in New York. I am a marcher for women's rights, climate change, and gun control. A natural consequence of this awakening was to express my outlook and outrage in my weaving.

The table runner entitled *Nevertheless She Persisted* resulted from my desire to add to my skill level in weaving by designing and weaving letters. An admirer of Senator Elizabeth Warren, I was outraged by the suppression of Senator Warren's speech in Congress in February 2017.

The colors chosen represent the black-and-white political climate that does not allow for factual discourse or shades of gray (compromise). Pink, the color of the hats worn in the Women's Marches, symbolizes the need for more women to speak out and stand up.

Beth MacVittie graduated from the Highland Hospital School of Nursing and worked in Boston, Boise, and Spokane before settling in the Rochester area. Most of her nursing career was in perioperative nursing at Strong Memorial Hospital. She has a biology degree from SUNY Geneseo and a master's in gerontological nursing from the University of Rochester. Retired from nursing, she is currently a massage therapist. An avid outdoors person, her interests include biking, kayaking, canoeing, hiking, and birding.

Beth's fiber interests were honed by her maternal grandmother who taught in a one-room schoolhouse. She taught Beth to sew, knit, and crochet when she was a child. Beth has been spinning yarn for thirty-five years. She also comes from a line of "hookers": her grandmother and mother were rug hookers, and Beth has joined their ranks. Currently, her favorite fiber endeavor is weaving. She has been taking weaving classes at the Weaving and Fiber Arts Center in East Rochester for five years. Her guild memberships include the Genesee Valley Handspinner's Guild, the Rochester Knitting Guild, and the Weavers' Guild of Rochester.

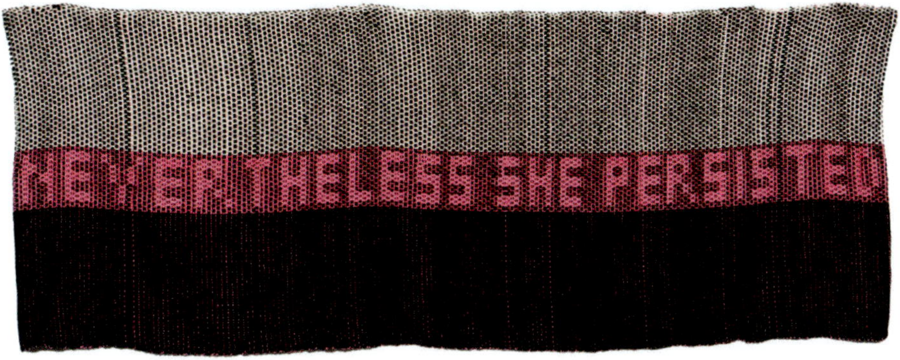
NEVERTHELESS SHE PERSISTED

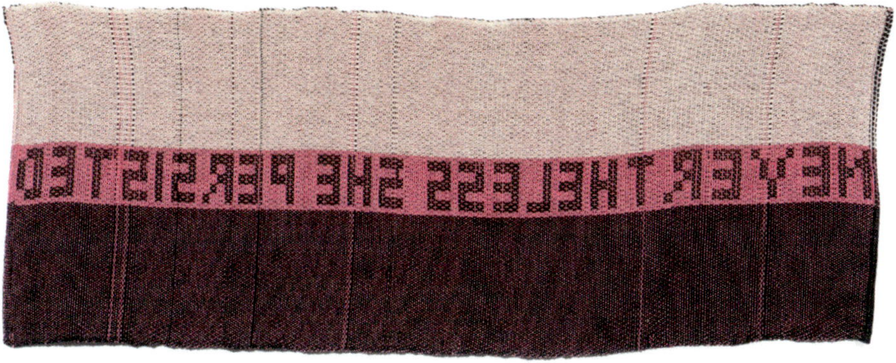

Katrina Majkut
DIY Counted Cross-Stitch Woman Card Kit

2017 / Aida cloth, needle, DMC floss, sassy instructions (English and Spanish), and a business card—all inside an archival plastic sleeve. Not included in kit: a personal sense of humor or political and personal outrage, scissors, embroidery hoop / 8.5 x 11"

The *DIY Counted Cross-Stitch Woman Card Kit* (2017) is a chance for embroiderers and concerned citizens to stab out stereotypes through needle art when it comes to the treatment of women and the challenges they face today. Katrina Majkut's cross-stitch kit attempts to insert feminism, humor, and politics into contemporary mass-produced kits that continue to assert cross-stitch as a passive, stereotypically gendered, and conservative domestic craft. By encouraging creators to express cathartically their individual and unique concerns, outrage, observations, and more, and then stitch them onto their own handmade cards, the project embraces the power of intersectionality and heightens the importance and power of the personal. As a limited edition, the kit can be used or kept intact as a work of fine art.

Katrina Majkut, a visual artist and writer, is dedicated to understanding how social traditions impact civil rights. She was listed by Mic Media as one of four international artists starting a new chapter in feminist art and was listed as a must-see artist by *Hyperallergic* magazine. Majkut specializes in feminism and Western wedding traditions, which are addressed in her nonfiction book, *The Adventures and Discoveries of a Feminist Bride* (Black Rose Writing). She recently did an Instagram art takeover for Planned Parenthood; exhibited at Spring Break, A.I.R. Gallery, Victori + Mo Gallery, CUNY College of Staten Island, Babson College, and the Mint Museum; and was an artist in residence at MASS MoCA. Her art catalogue is in the library at the National Museum of Women in the Arts, DC.

CONNECT

www.KatrinaMajkut.com
Twitter: @KatrinaMajkut
Instagram: @KatrinaMajkut

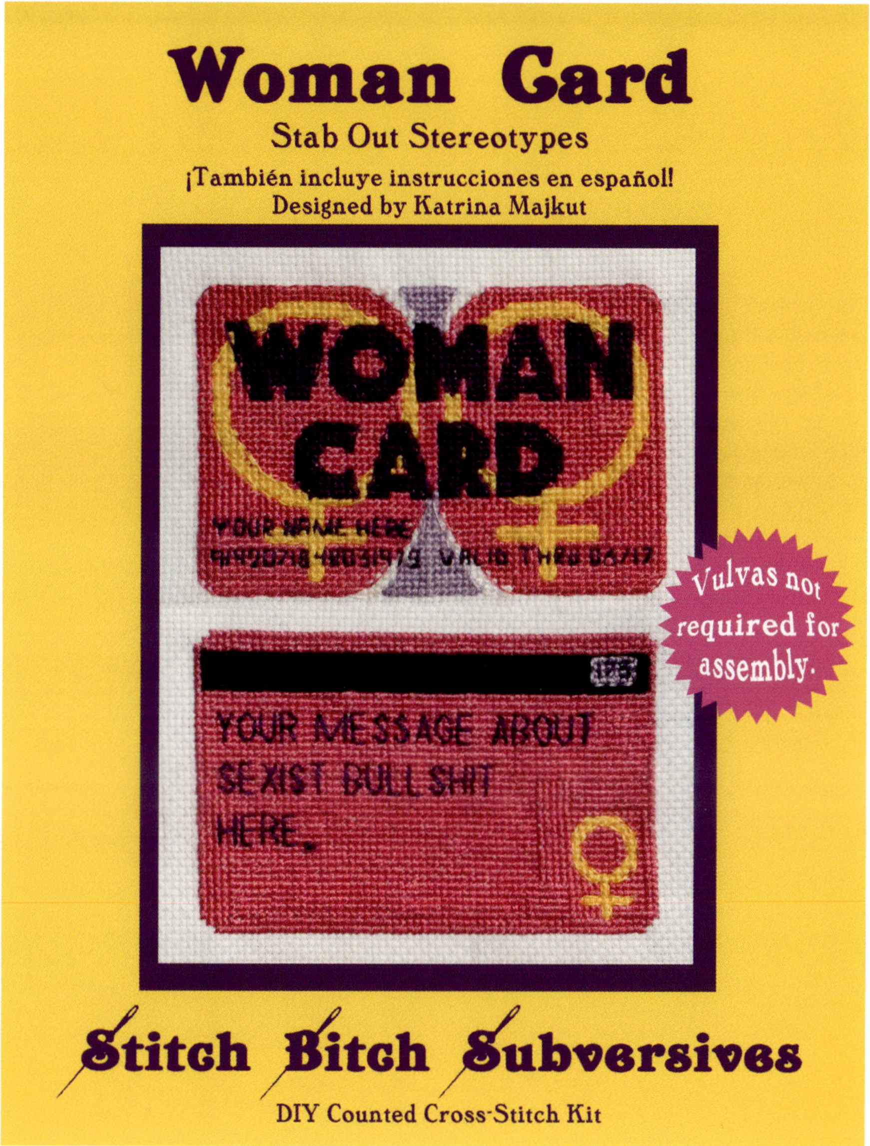
Woman Card
Stab Out Stereotypes
¡También incluye instrucciones en español!
Designed by Katrina Majkut
WOMAN
CARD
YOUR NAME HERE
YOUR MESSAGE ABOUT
SEXIST BULLSHIT
HERE.
Vulvas not required for assembly.
Stitch Bitch Subversives
DIY Counted Cross-Stitch Kit

Hinda Mandell

Which Hat Is Which? Pussy Hat, the Original Pussyhat, Dunce Cap, Drumpf Hat, Make America Great Again Hat

2018 / Wool yarn, acrylic yarn, cotton embroidery floss, plastic toy eyes, kids' hair embellishments / The five hats, when lined up together, measure 4 x 12"

This artwork interrogates the role of hats in American political culture, examines how hats are used to indicate political and identity allegiances, and also explores how hats have been used to discipline people who step out of line. This work's title is intended to provoke discussion among viewers: What is the original "pussy" hat? Is it the bright pink hat that millions wore on January 21, 2017, during the Women's March and in subsequent protest marches, or is it a KKK hood, for instance, offering a play on the word *pussy* (someone who's a coward, and who would need to cover his face to engage in activities of hate). This work was created eighteen months after the first Women's March, after I'd had some time to ponder and mull over the power of words, and their implications, and their connection to headwear that orients people to their politics in a way that's public and provocative.

Hinda Mandell, PhD, is associate professor in the School of Communication at Rochester Institute of Technology and coeditor, along with Christine Kray and Tamar Carroll, of *Nasty Women & Bad Hombres: Gender and Race in the 2016 US Presidential Election* (University of Rochester Press, 2018); author of *Sex Scandals, Gender and Power in Contemporary American Politics* (Praeger, 2017); and coeditor, along with Gina Masullo Chen, of *Scandal in a Digital Age* (Palgrave Macmillan, 2016). She is under contract with Rowman & Littlefield to edit the essay collection *Crafting Dissent: Handicraft as Protest from the American Revolution to the Anti-Trump Pussyhats.*

CONNECT

omghinda.com

Twitter: @crochetactivism and @hindamandell

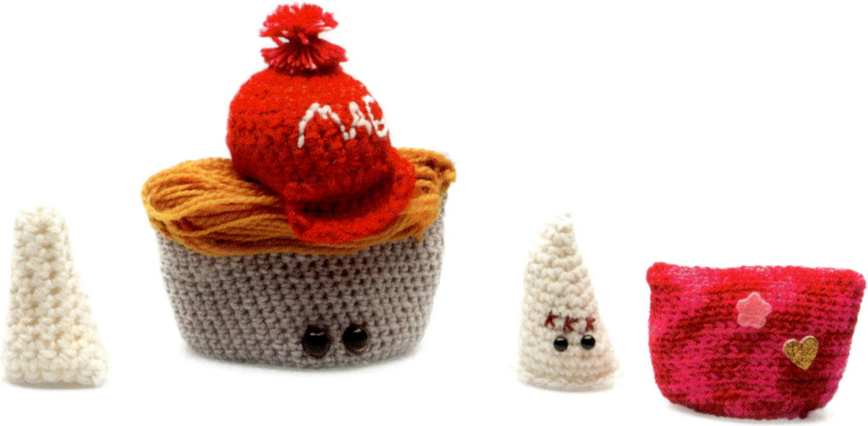

Kayla Mattes
UMP

2018 / Cotton and wool

UMP is a woven series that critiques our current president by playfully altering his name with repetitious rhyming that relates back to his character. GRUMP, CHUMP, DUMP—each word perfectly pokes fun at his idiocy. By embracing a juvenile sense of humor, *UMP* aims to fight the feeling of hopelessness and fear rampant in Trump's America through silly, yet powerful, acts of rebellion. The flat color, graphic lettering, and fringed edges of the woven cloth suggest each piece is a scarf or a banner. When reading the text, you can hear the people chant together, not words of support but of opposition.

Kayla Mattes is a visual artist working across disciplines, including weaving, sculpture, and installation. She archives the ephemeral vernacular of digital culture through the interconnected threads of tapestry, crafting sly political jabs through repetitive language and familiar symbols. Recent exhibitions include *POST* (Los Angeles), Cal State, Channel Islands (Camarillo, CA), *Tiger Strikes Ahead*, Philadelphia, FISK Gallery (Portland, OR), LVL3 (Chicago), Disjecta Contemporary Art Center (Portland, OR), Border Patrol Gallery (Portland, ME), and Hunter College (NYC). Her work has been featured in *Maake* magazine, i-D, Rhizome, and *Sculpture* magazine, and was included in the 2018 book *Weavers: Contemporary Makers on the Loom*, written by Katie Tregidden and published by Ludion. She received a BFA in textiles at Rhode Island School of Design in 2011 and an MFA from the University of California, Santa Barbara in 2019.

CONNECT

www.kaylamattes.com
Instagram: @kaylamattes

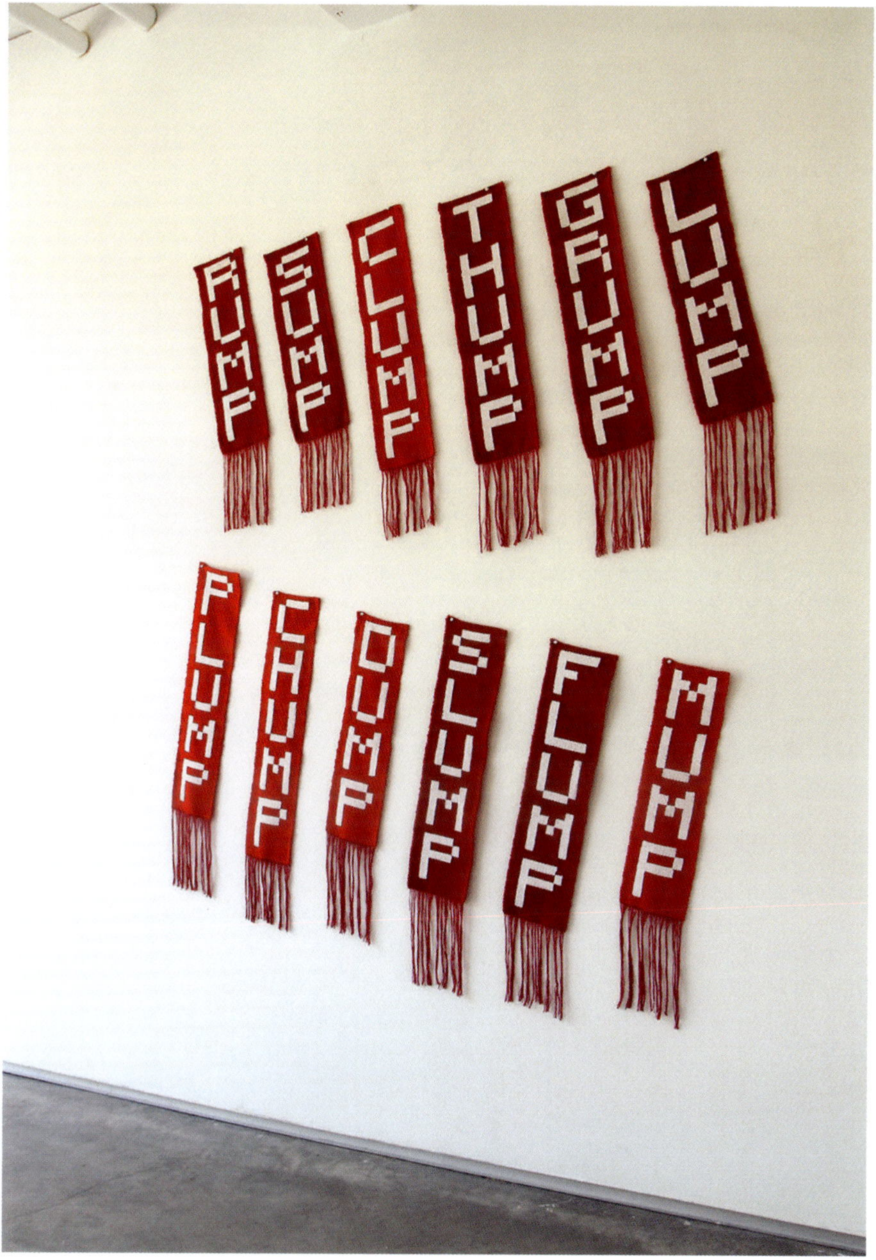
RUMP
SUMP
CLUMP
THUMP
GRUMP
LUMP
PLUMP
CHUMP
DUMP
SLUMP
FLUMP
MUMP

Joetta Maue
Mother and Child

2018 / Cotton embroidery floss, found linen / 44 x 50"

I view motherhood as a political act. Mothers are left out of art history, the job market, and the dialogue of equal rights, even in the community of women. Mothers are a voice that is often stifled and ignored. My work explores the dynamic, conflicting emotions of the mother as she finds her own identity and struggles with it, all while caring for and loving her children. My image-based work explores the physical space and experience of these relationships, while my text-based work explores the complicated emotions that reside within intimacy and identity. My embroidered drawings allow me to zoom in on the importance of the small, possibly insignificant, moments of domesticity and focus on their texture, tones, and detail, abstracting their meaning and role while simultaneously elevating them. My studio practice involves labor-intensive techniques that force me to work slowly, meticulously, and daily on my art. The finished work becomes a map of daily life. Though the autobiographical drives the work and is necessary for it to exist, ultimately it is transcended, enabling the viewers to have their own independent relationship to the work. The goal is to no longer ignore or romanticize motherhood, but to share it as a valid and valuable subject of the human experience in art.

Joetta Maue is an artist, curator, and arts writer. Joetta received her BFA from The Ohio State University and her MFA from the University of Massachusetts Amherst. Joetta's work has been shown throughout galleries and museums across the country and internationally. Joetta authored the studio blog *Little Yellowbird,* and is a freelance curator and a regular contributor to a number of journals. She has been featured in numerous books and journals, including *Indie Craft, PUSH Stitchery, Needle Magazine, Fiber Arts Now, Martha Stewart Living,* and the *Surface Design Journal.* She is a lecturer in the photography department at UMass Boston, lecturer at Northeastern University and Massachusetts College of Art, and an invited instructor at a number of programs and institutions across the country. Joetta lives in New England with her family.

CONNECT

www.joettamaue.com
Instagram: @joettamaue

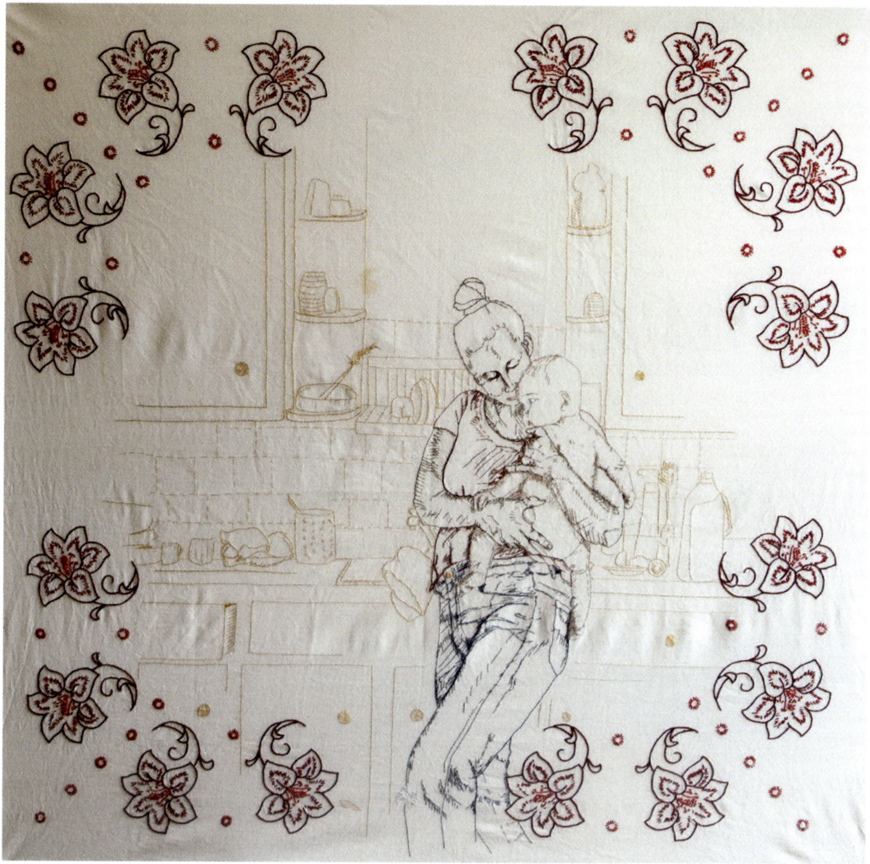

Nanci Nugent
Black Doll in Plaid Dress

2017 / Osnaburg, paint, stuffing, homespun, cotton embroidery / 19 x 8″

Our complex and fast world too often focuses on how quickly a product can be manufactured or consumed in the shortest amount of time. This fast culture gives little thought to sustainability or to the people creating the items. The result may be feelings of isolation.

A handmade item such as a doll provided children comfort during frightening times in our country, during slavery and now in the present time, when many may not feel comfortable in our society. This African American doll looks very much like dolls made by African American women in the 1850s through the 1940s. The doll exhibited here was influenced by the book *Black Dolls: Unique African American Dolls, 1850–1930*, from the collection of Deborah Neff.

Our country is diverse, with immigrants and migrants arriving every day. All races and cultures need to be represented, thereby promoting democracy. We all look different, but we all really want the same things: safety, love, and freedom.

Nanci Nugent is from Westchester County, New York. She would often take the train to the museums in New York City, where she was introduced to the world of art and art history. She now lives in Scottsville, New York, and has been a librarian for more than thirty years. She is an art librarian at the Central Library of Rochester and Monroe County, where she oversees the Arts and Literature Division. Nanci has a degree in art history from the State University of New York at Brockport and a master's in library science from the State University of New York at Buffalo.

Nanci taught herself how to sew and has been making her own clothing for about twenty years and dolls for about fifteen. She is also a printmaker and has made books for *Art of the Book* at the Central Library. She teaches printmaking classes in engraving and monotype printing at the Central Library, and has also taught doll-making classes. She also taught herself how to crochet and has done yarnbombing outside the library along Broad Street.

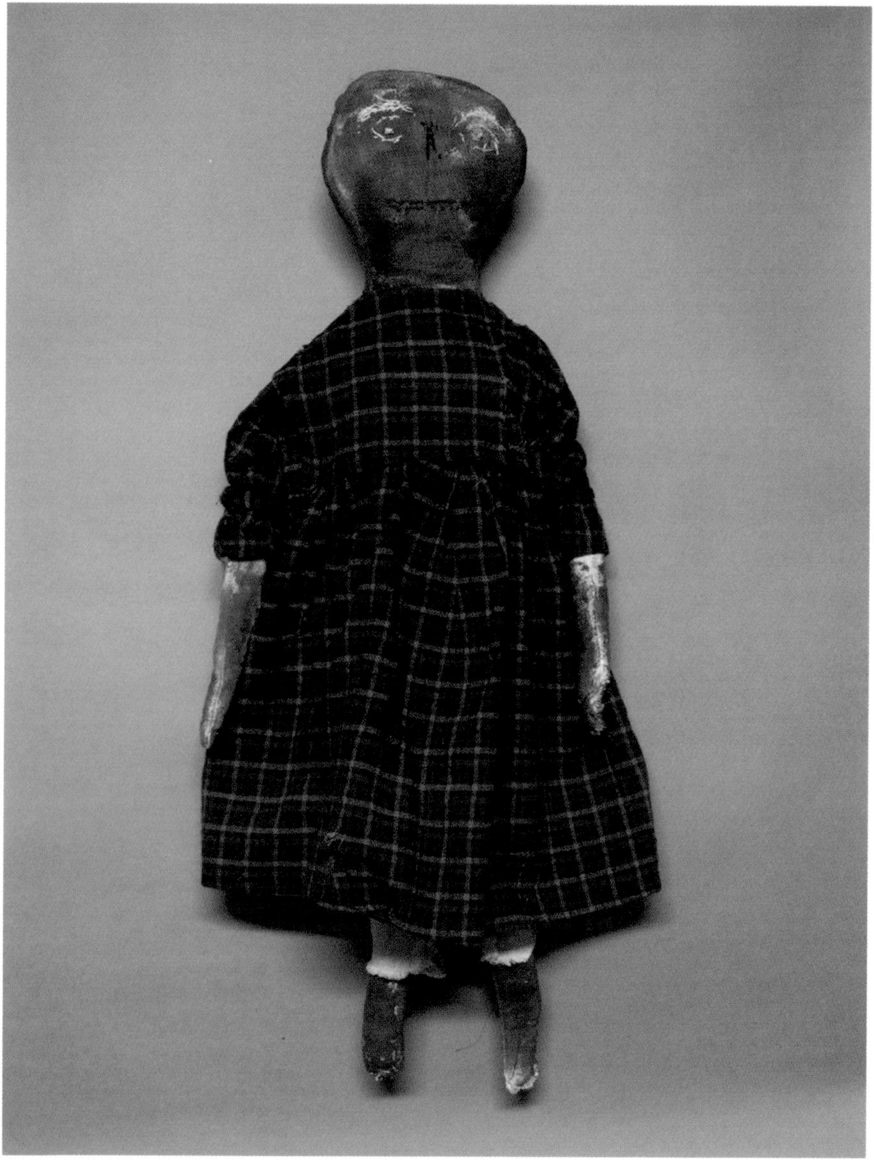

Alfonse Pagano
Twelve Plus One

2018 / Deconstructed American flag / 60 x 132"

As an artist and a maker of things, I am attempting to express my deepest sorrow and pain, my shock and disbelief regarding what is happening right now, through my work. I have turned to the most obvious symbol to express these feelings: the American flag. In a series of images, I have deconstructed it and ripped it apart. The flag becomes a relic—ruined, torn, and battered. These images are part of a series entitled *Rush to Relics*. It is my interpretation of the recent violations of the Constitution and destruction of vitally important programs in the United States as it relates to and impacts the common citizen under the Trump administration.

In my deconstruction and manipulation of the American flag, I intend to transform the flag into something physically and emotionally separate from its previous pristine, iconic state, distinct from its origin, as a way to express the current and toxic political climate.

The flags are first distressed, aged, and torn apart. Then I reconstruct them in three-dimensional form, and some in collage form, which are photographs printed on rice paper and laminated to canvas. For the collages, I further work them with pen, paint, and graphite. These manipulations take the flag farther away from its crisp, clean, and pure state.

Alfonse Pagano's background has its roots in fine art. A recipient of several grants, including the New York Foundation for the Arts, he has exhibited his mixed media and oil works at the Carnegie Mellon Museum of Art and the Laguna Gloria Museum of Art, as well as many galleries throughout the US. Following an inspired idea, he embarked on a project that took him around the world. The result was a collaborative compilation of images and interviews of people from all walks of life delivering a personal philosophy behind their dreadlocks. In 1999, the photo-documentary book *Dreads* was published by Artisan/Workman. Currently in its eighth printing, *Dreads* has earned both national and international acclaim, with exhibits at the Wadsworth Atheneum Museum of Art, University of Maryland, Paterson Museum, and Stevens Institute, and recently as a subject featured on NPR.

CONNECT

www.alfonsepaganowork.com
https://www.facebook.com/alfonse.pagano
Instagram: @apagano09

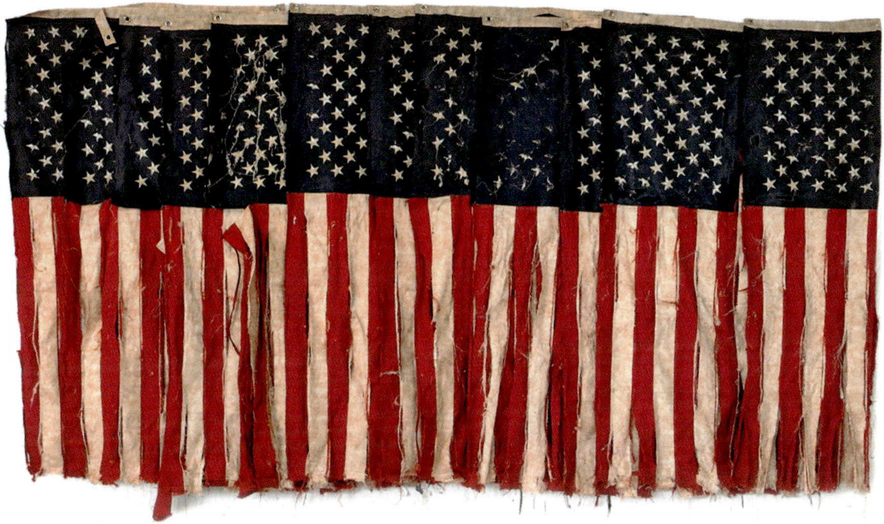

Kathryn Pellman
Love Wins!

2015 / Dupioni silk, commercial cottons, metallic fabric, cotton and rayon thread, fabric paint / 18 x 13"

Love Wins! is a celebration of marriage equality. I was overjoyed to wake up on the morning of June 26, 2015, to the news that same-sex couples could marry in all fifty states. I think Justice Anthony Kennedy said it best when he wrote, "The Court now holds that same-sex couples may exercise the fundamental right to marry." The heart is Keith Haring-inspired.

Kathryn Pellman is a Los Angeles artist, fashionista, quilter, cook, baker, gardener, and storyteller. Her whimsical quilts combine fashion and quilting, along with her passion to create single-frame cartoon stories that invoke fashion illustration and feature mostly long-limbed and knobby-kneed female figures she calls "fashionistas." She describes her semi-autobiographical quilts as a celebration and exploration of women and femininity. Her newest series *Angry Nasty Women*, is how she expresses her views and feelings about the issues that impact all of us as Americans. Her quilts have been exhibited throughout the United States and have been written about in the *New York Times* and the *Los Angeles Times*. Kathryn recently taped three segments for *Quilting Arts TV* and is the coauthor of *Backart: On the Flip Side*.

CONNECT

KathrynPellman.com

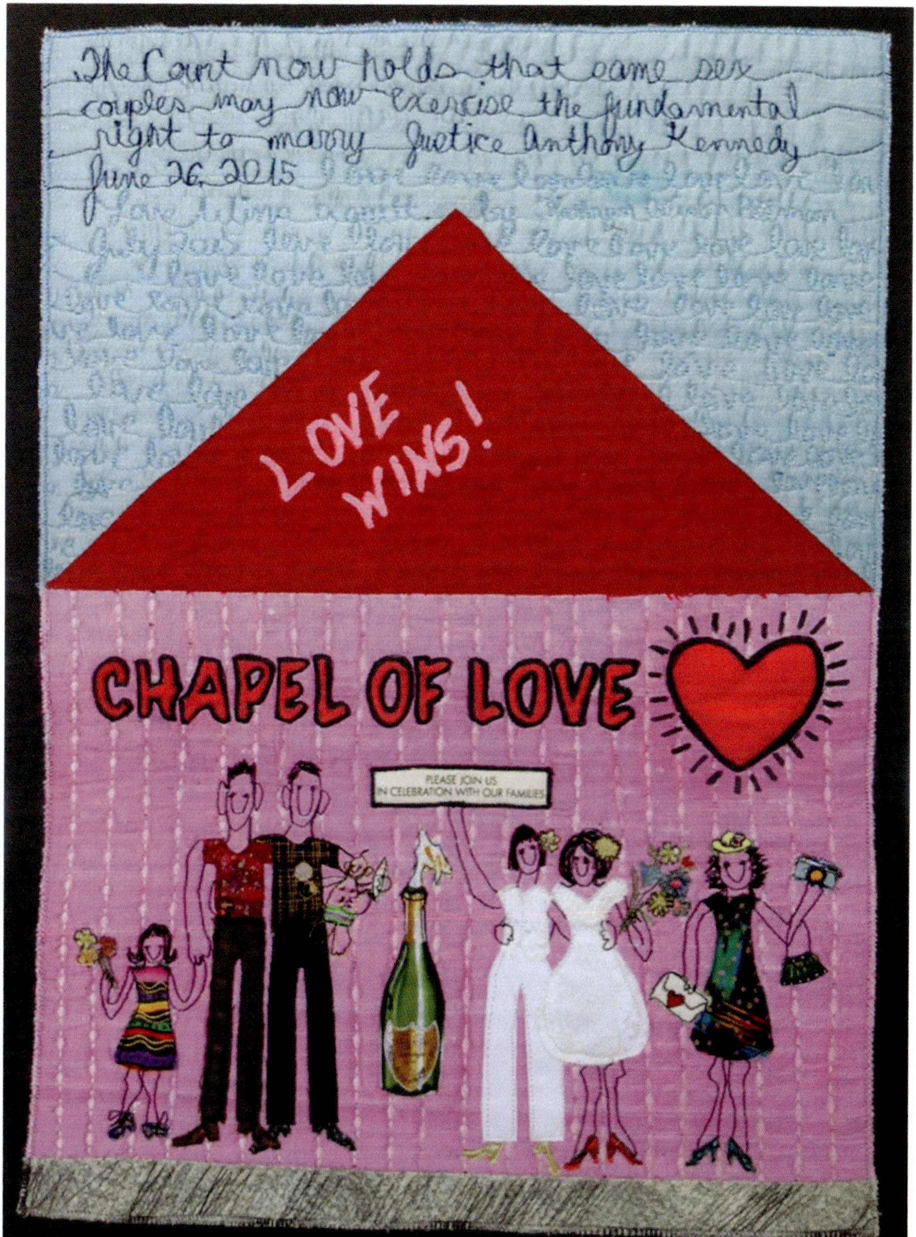
The Court now holds that same sex
couples may now exercise the fundamental
right to marry Justice Anthony Kennedy
June 26, 2015
LOVE WINS!
CHAPEL OF LOVE
PLEASE JOIN US
IN CELEBRATION WITH OUR FAMILIES

Jessica M. Skultety
Hear Our Voice

2017 / Cotton fabric with cotton thread / 36 x 43"

Hear Our Voice was sewn in one week and held proudly as a protest banner at the Women's March on Washington, DC, on January 21, 2017. This is one of several quilts Skultety has made in response to the results of the 2016 election. Since quilts have a long history of association with American politics, as well as objects of comfort, using them to discuss and engage in current political discourse—anything but comfortable—seems like common sense. The quilt is made to be inclusive of women all over the world; the words "Our Health Matters" bring attention to the often disregarded importance of a woman's choice and well-being. The back states, "LOVE," which was hand stitched onto a vibrant rainbow background while en route to DC. It is meant to show solidarity with the LGBTQ+ community. The aftereffects of making this quilt have been overwhelming excitement and support at the march and in its travels.

Jessica M. Skultety of Phillipsburg, New Jersey, is a quilter, teacher, and lecturer. Her quilts have been featured in many venues, including International Quilt Festival, QuiltCon, Road to California, AIR Gallery, Ontario Museum of History & Art, and a solo exhibition at the 2017 Quilt and Sewing Fest of New Jersey. Currently, she is a featured artist with the Fuller Craft Museum in Brockton, Massachusetts, creating art to bring attention to the opioid epidemic. Jessica served as the president, vice president, and webmaster of the nonprofit Central Jersey Modern Quilt Guild. A self-taught quilter, she focuses on empowering the sewing community online and in person to take risks with their sewing.

CONNECT

www.quiltyhabit.com
Instagram: @quiltyhabit

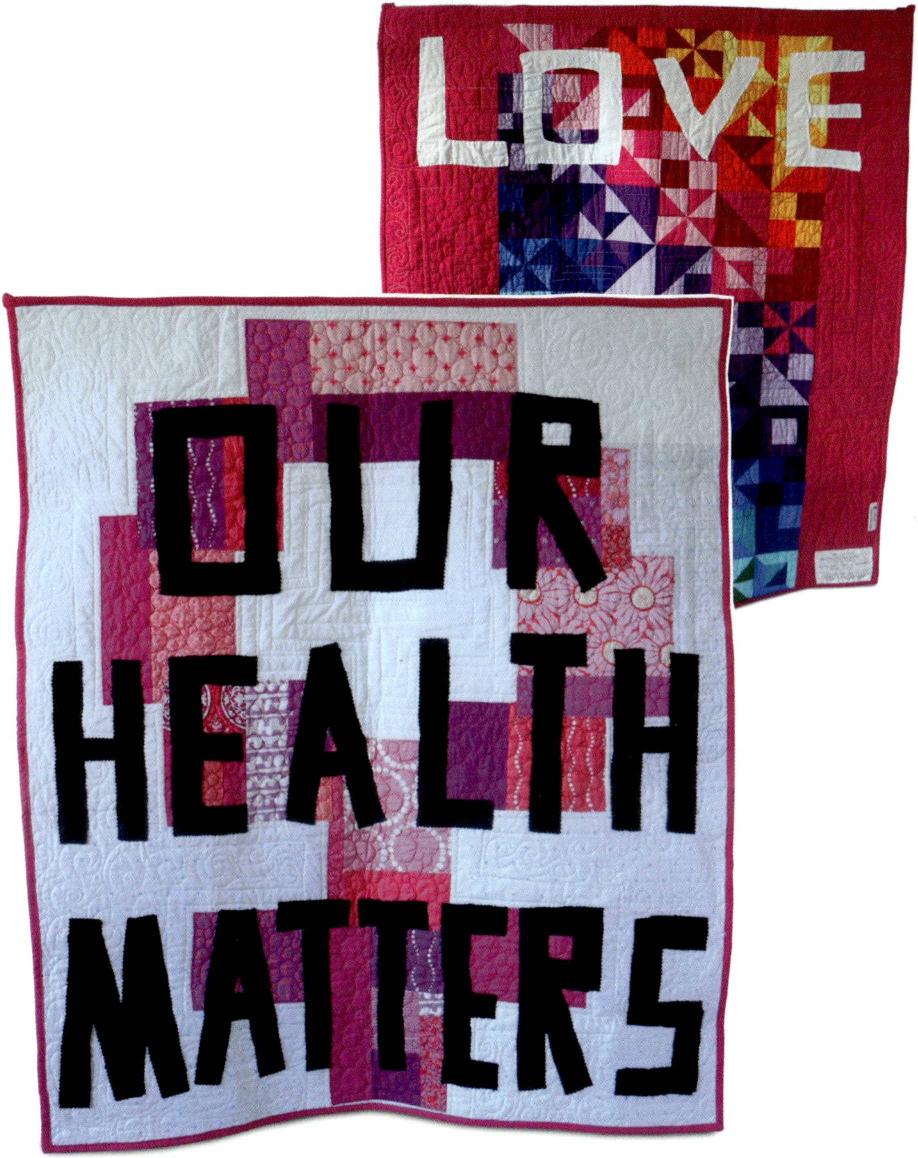
LOVE
OUR
HEALTH
MATTERS

Adrienne Sloane
The Unraveling

2017 / Cotton knit, poly and cotton fabrics / 73 x 38 x 8"

As I listen to the news while in my studio, I often find myself responding viscerally to the political landscape of the day. The news has been dominated since 2017 by an unorthodox administration that I see as undermining our democracy, national unity, and the values we stand for as Americans. Using an iconic national symbol, *The Unraveling* is the third in a series of flags that I have created over the last ten years. I will continue to unravel this piece—set against the backdrop of the Constitution, which is increasingly revealed—according to the timeline of the current administration as long as our civil and political rights continue to erode.

A contemporary fiber artist with a political focus, Adrienne Sloane deeply explores all forms of sculptural knit structures out of her Massachusetts studio. As a hand and machine knitter, she often addresses timely but universal issues in her work, while remaining mindful of the rich historical context of her medium. Sloane exhibits and teaches internationally and has also worked with indigenous knitters on economic development projects in Bolivia and Peru. Sloane has work in major collections and has been published widely. She also enjoys writing regularly for the magazine *Fiber Art Now*.

CONNECT

www.adriennesloane.com
Instagram: @adrienne_sloane

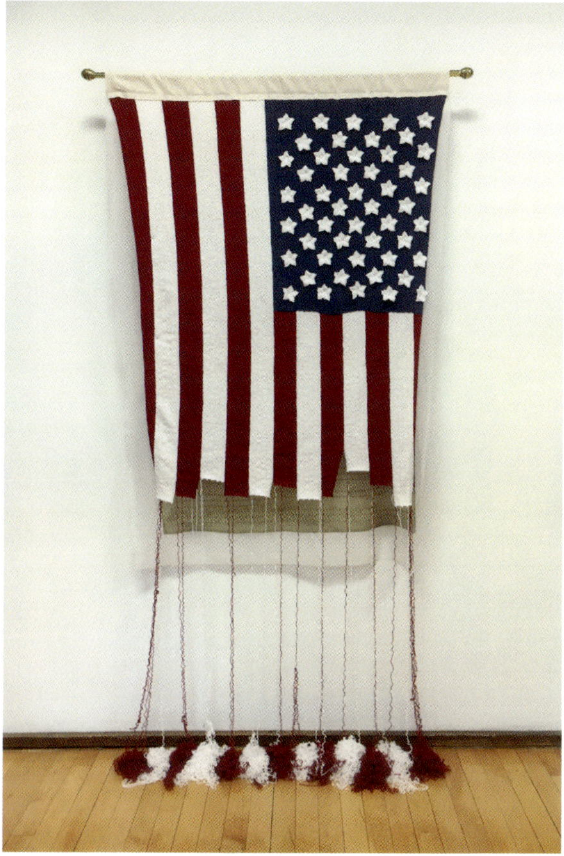

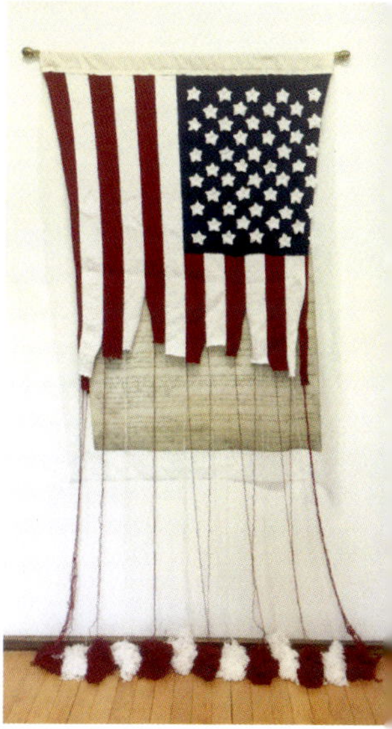

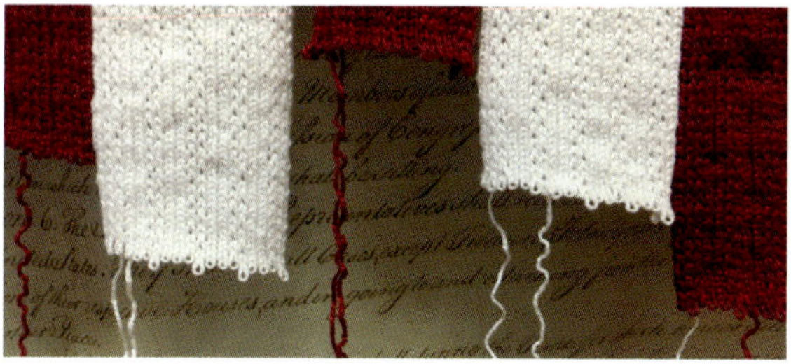

Adrienne Sloane
Games People Play

2018 / Free motion quilting, cotton / 35 x 40.5″

Games People Play is a triptych commenting on various aspects of the Trump presidency in the form of word games.

Part 1: *Seven Dirty Words: CDC Anagram*

Seven Dirty Words is a takeoff on George Carlin's 1972 monologue "Seven Words You Can Never Say on Television," which used words that at the time were considered too controversial for broadcast. While in 2018 avoiding controversial words may have been a strategy by the Centers for Disease Control and Prevention to improve the chances of funding from an increasingly right-leaning administration, the analogy strongly holds.

Part 2: *Know Their Names: Groper Word Search*

Know Their Names is a word search that includes the names of the eighteen women who accused Donald Trump of groping them. Trump's name, as well as the phrases "Locker Room Talk" and "Grab 'Em by the Pussy," are also included.

Part 3: *Eyes on the Lies: 100 Days of Fictionary*

Eyes on the Lies is taken from a graphic in the *Washington Post* that lays out in calendar form the number of lies Trump told on each of his first 100 days in office. Normally considered the honeymoon period, as of day 100, he had made 492 false or misleading claims. The graphic, along with more detailed information, can be found at https://www.washingtonpost.com/graphics/politics/trump-claims/

A contemporary fiber artist with a political focus, Adrienne Sloane deeply explores all forms of sculptural knit structures out of her Massachusetts studio. As a hand and machine knitter, she often addresses timely but universal issues in her work while remaining mindful of the rich historical context of her medium. Sloane exhibits and teaches internationally and has also worked with indigenous knitters on economic development projects in Bolivia and Peru. Sloane has work in major collections and has been published widely. She also enjoys writing regularly for the magazine *Fiber Art Now*.

CONNECT

www.adriennesloane.com
Instagram: @adrienne_sloane

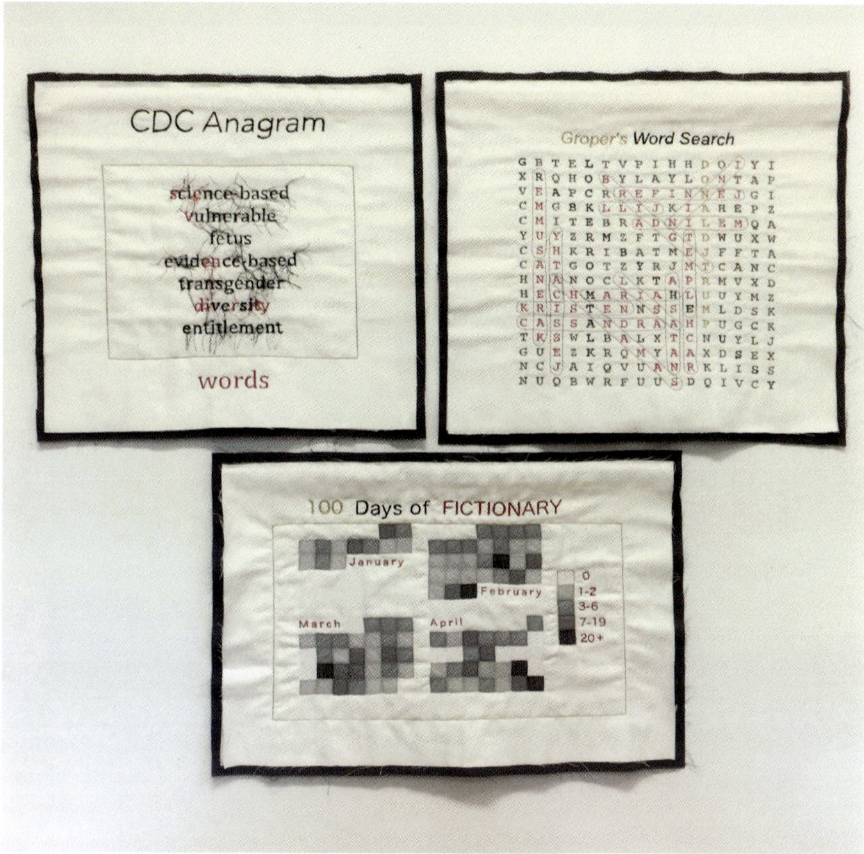
CDC Anagram
science-based
vulnerable
fetus
evidence-based
transgender
diversity
entitlement
words
Groper's Word Search
100 Days of FICTIONARY
January
February
March
April
0
1-2
3-6
7-19
20+

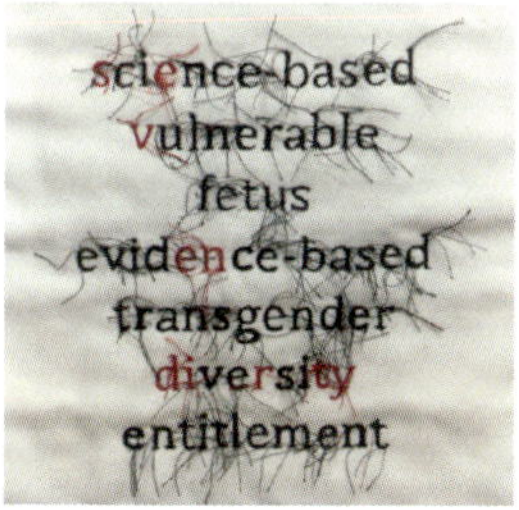
science-based
vulnerable
fetus
evidence-based
transgender
diversity
entitlement

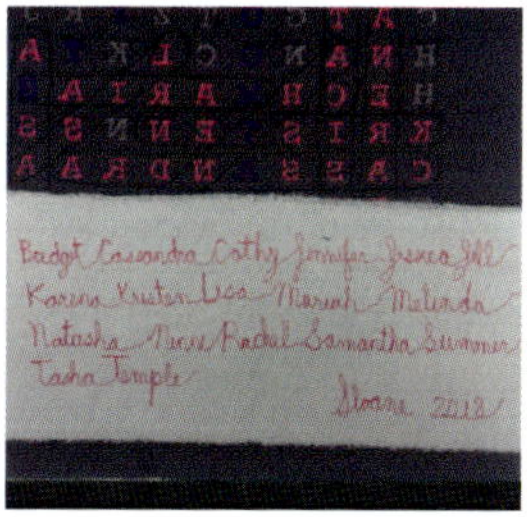

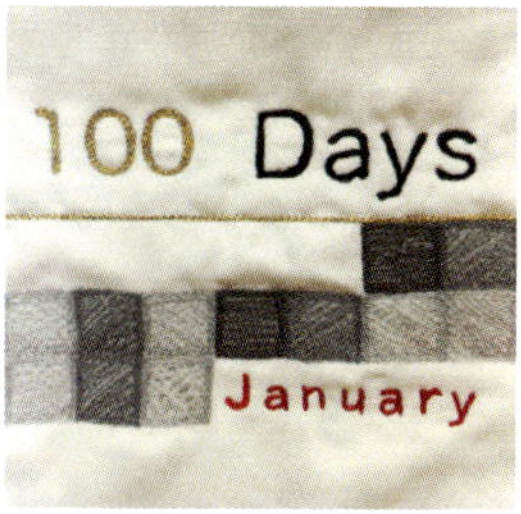
100 Days
January

Jill St. Coeur

Just Rewards (a series of three pieces: *Break the Glass Ceiling, Run for Prez, Equal Pay for Equal Work*)

2016 / New and recycled wool on a linen backing / Each piece is 20 x 20"

This series is a reaction to the 2016 presidential debates between Donald Trump and Hillary Clinton. The artist's inspiration came from embracing the reality that it was time to have a woman as president of our country. The pieces' titles reflect the women's issues that were rising to the surface during the campaign, such as *Break the Glass Ceiling*, *Running for Prez*, and *Equal Pay for Equal Work*. The use of the traditional women's art of rug hooking conveys "the confluence of craft, art, and activism" that is the rationale for this exhibit.

Jill St. Coeur received her undergraduate degree in costume design, clothing, and textiles, and earned her graduate degree in clothing and human behavior. She has designed costumes for theater and dance both nationally and internationally. She continues to work from her studio, designing and creating custom clothing, and exhibiting her hooked rugs throughout the US.

CONNECT

jillstcoeurartrugs.com
www.facebook.com/jill.coeur

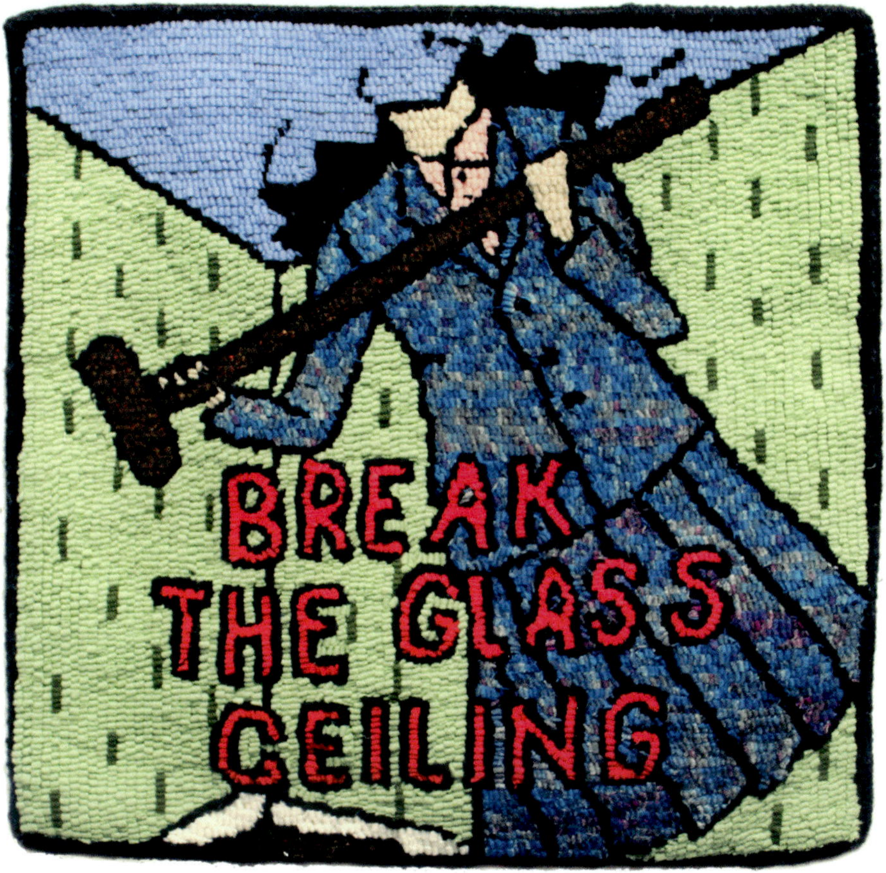
BREAK
THE GLASS
CEILING

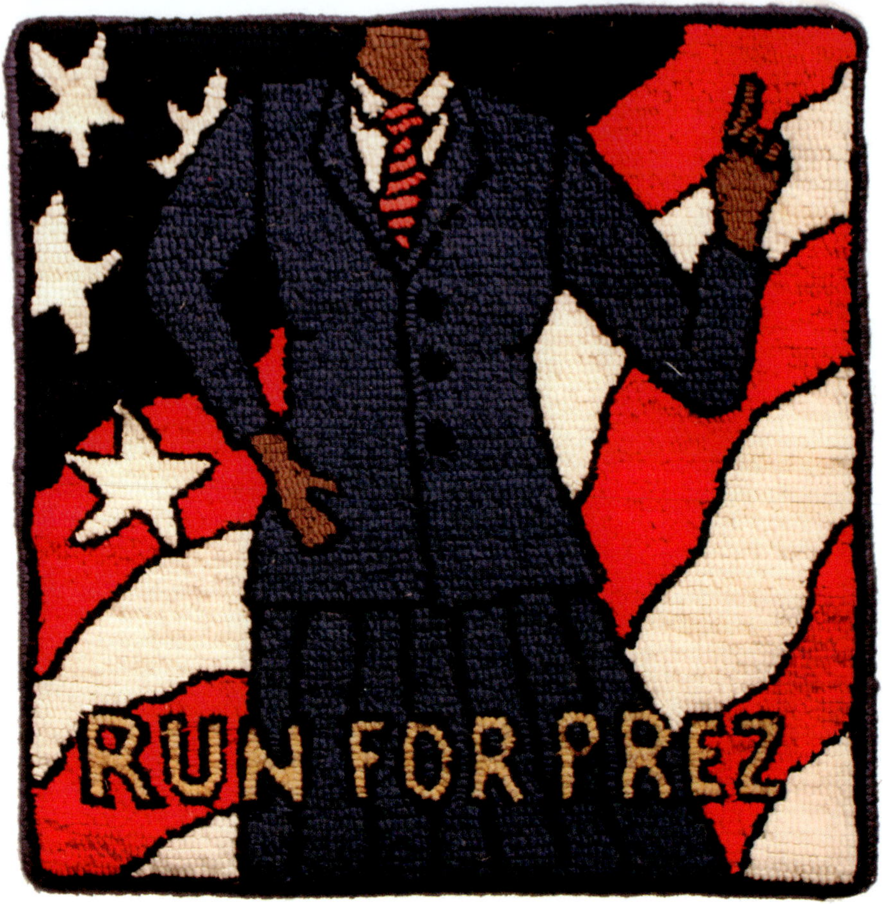
RUN FOR PREZ

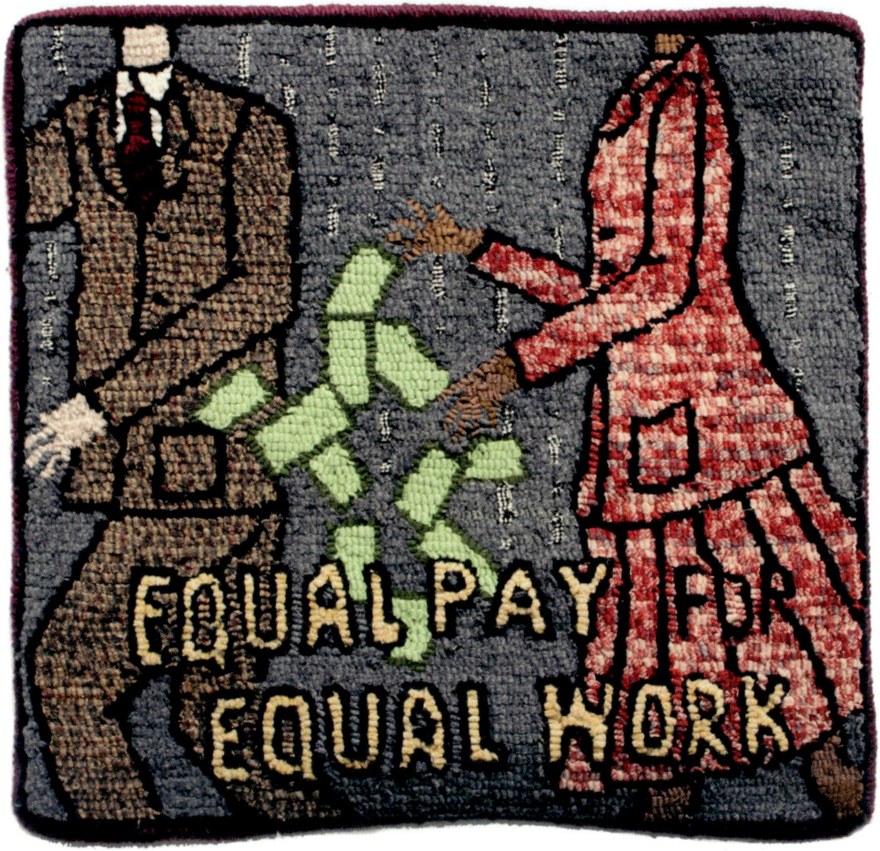
EQUAL PAY FOR
EQUAL WORK

Kathy A. Suprenant
Un-word of the Year

2018 / Cotton fabrics and embroidery threads, oil paint sticks / 28.5 x 19.25 x 1.5"

In January 2018, a panel of German linguists selected *alternative Fakten* as the "Un-word of the Year," describing the phrase as a "disguised and misleading term for the attempt to make false claims acceptable as a legitimate means for public debate." Truthiness, doublespeak, and alternative facts: When did we, as United Statesians, normalize deception and dishonesty?

In this quilt, Kellyanne Conway, Counselor to the President, attends the 2017 presidential inauguration in "Trump revolutionary wear." Strolling among a series of notable quotes from former White House Press Secretary Sean Spicer, NBC reporter Chuck Todd, and herself, Kellyanne ushers in an era of Trumpian truthlessness. She emerges, or perhaps escapes, from a sea of appliquéd clamshells, rendered in dark blue to symbolize trust, loyalty, and truth.

Un-word of the Year belongs to the quilt series *What Did Ming Miss?* Ming is a nickname for a 507-year-old Icelandic clam (circa 1499–2006) that was "born" during the Ming Dynasty, captured alive, and subsequently died. Initially, I focused on playful topics translated in bright colors in a naive art style. As the tumultuous US presidential primary and election came to pass, the subject matter changed to reflect the attitudes of an anxious, frustrated, and perhaps bamboozled nation.

Kathy Suprenant grew up in the village of Hudson Falls in northern New York and is proud to be a first-generation college graduate. She received a BS in biology from the State University of New York at Albany and a PhD in biology from the University of Virginia in Charlottesville. In 2016, Kathy retired as professor emeritus in the Department of Molecular Biosciences at the University of Kansas. While at KU, Kathy served as department chair, taught cell biology, and published original research on the role of the cytoskeleton in cell division and early development. Kathy retired early to concentrate on a fiber art career. Most of her work is meticulously hand appliquéd, elaborately embellished, and often assembled into three-dimensional arrays. It is a leisurely process that connects her physically (her DNA is on every fiber) and emotionally to many serious and whimsical topics of interest.

CONNECT

kathysuprenant.com

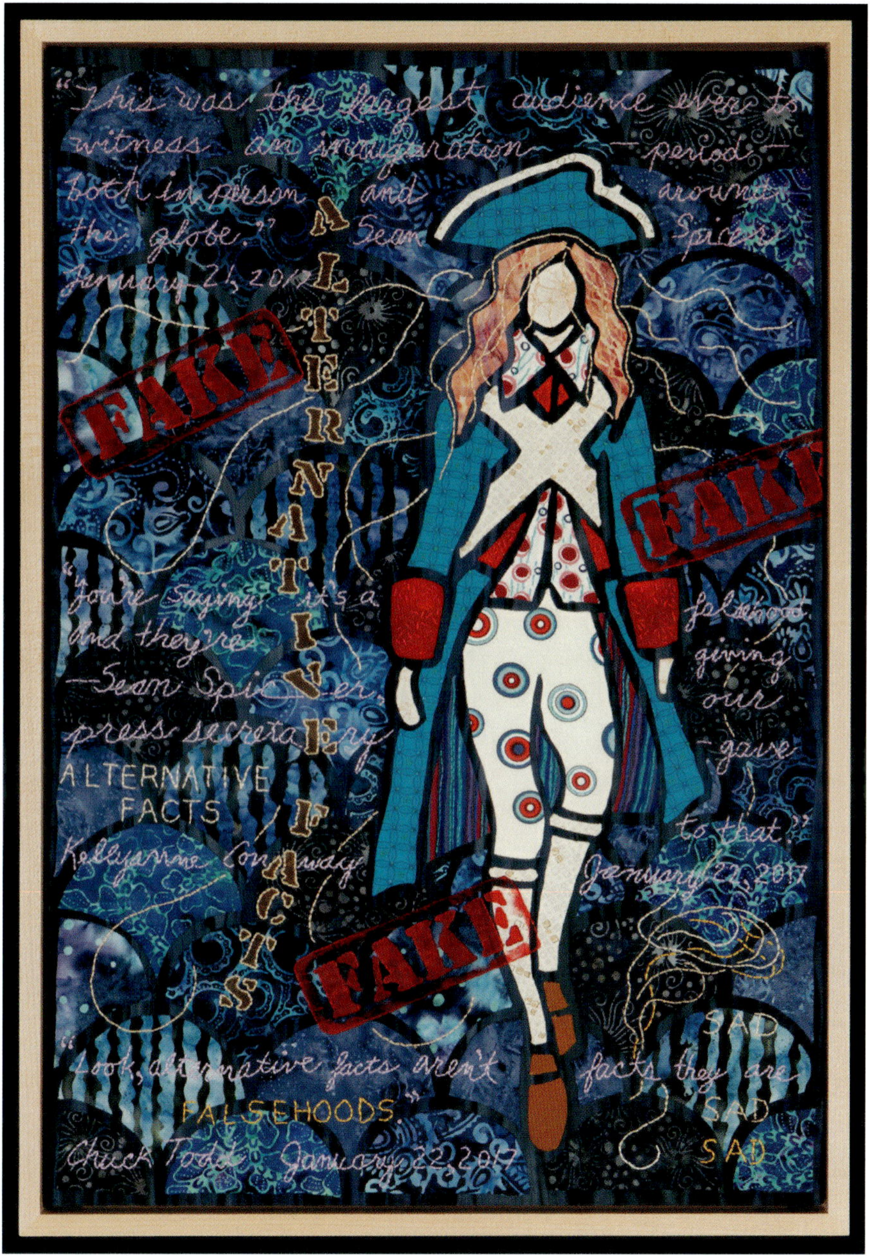

"This was the largest audience ever to witness an inauguration — period — both in person and around the globe." Sean Spicer January 21, 2017
ALTERNATIVE FACTS
FAKE
FAKE
FAKE
FAKE
"You're saying it's a falsehood. And they're giving our —Sean Spicer, press secretary — gave ALTERNATIVE FACTS to that" Kellyanne Conway January 22, 2017
"Look, alternative facts aren't facts, they are FALSEHOODS" Chuck Todd January 22, 2017
SAD
SAD
SAD

Melanie Tuazon
Women's Work

2016–17 / Cotton fabric, linen fabric, cotton batting, cotton thread / 71 x 71"

Women's Work is a quilt depicting the highest and hardest glass ceiling, cracked but unbroken in the aftermath of the 2016 election. It is an object of comfort made from the collective heartbreak of that loss, and a metaphor for ambition made using a traditionally domestic practice. Twelve women representing different states, experiences, professions, and identities contributed improvised blocks that were sliced and combined into panes by Melanie Tuazon to celebrate individuality while also demonstrating unity and community. Collaborators, in alphabetical order, are: Jeanine Bowen, Aleeda Crawley, Sarah Fader, Ashley Hinton, Karin Jordan, Alyson Olander, Krishma Patel, Melissa Quaal, Michelle Reiter, Virginia Robinson, Anne Sullivan, and Kitty Wilkin. Each quilter contributed personal fabric, design elements or both, representing their feelings in a post-election America, including fabric turned wrong side out to symbolize our country going backward, prints representing makers' children, upcycled fabric for environmentalism, and pieced hearts broken in the process of assembly. The artists use "women's work" to address the topic of women in the workplace and the failure to achieve one of feminism's biggest goals, looking beyond heartbreak toward the work of the future.

Melanie Tuazon is a quilter, writer, and fiber artist. Her work has appeared in national quilt shows and traveled internationally with the Modern Quilt Guild's touring exhibits. She teaches workshops throughout the US, but calls the New Jersey suburbs home.

CONNECT

melintheattic.com
Instagram and Twitter:
@melintheattic

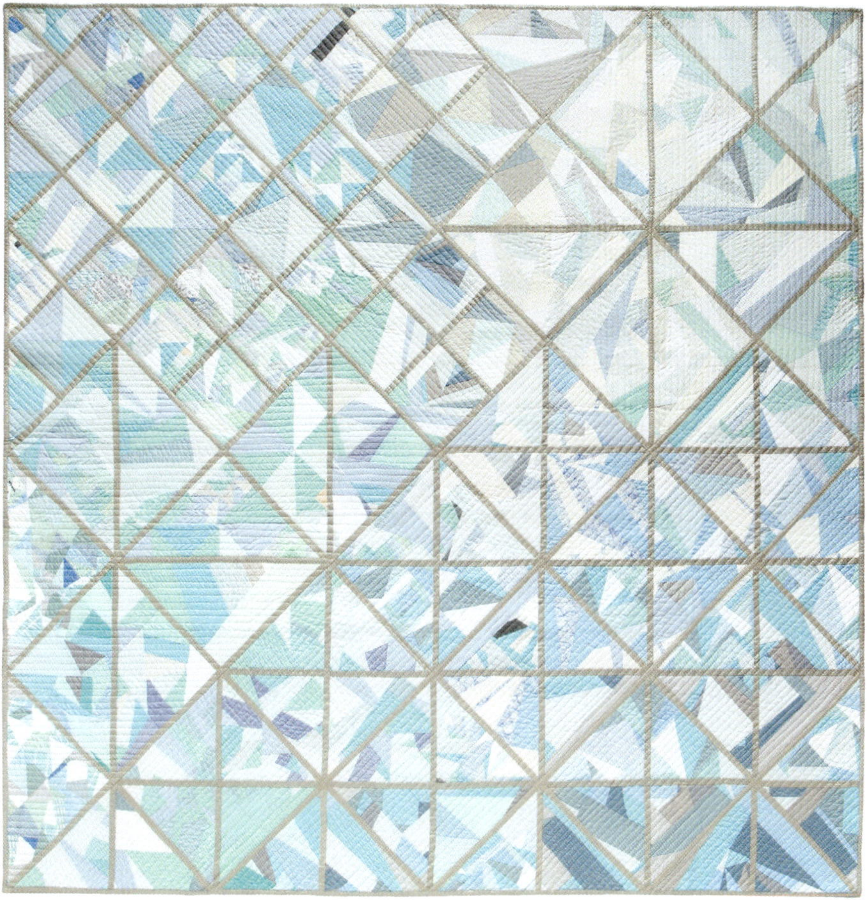

Kathy J. Weber
State of the Union

2017 / Wool weft on linen warp / 18.5 x 12.25"

We are all part of crafting our American democracy—every person living here in the United States—regardless of immigration or citizenship status. When I designed this piece, it was simply a statement of where we were: divided into red and blue states. My work acknowledges that geography, history, religion, social class, race, zoning, school districts, education, local culture, local beliefs, and individuality shape our views. The organizations that once were staples of national culture are connecting fewer and fewer people. Public schools, religious institutions, the armed services, organized sports, children's organizations, clubs, and volunteer organizations are experiencing downturns in involvement. Where once news came from networks touting their journalistic excellence, social media and media algorithms provide the news desired, instead of the news that is current. If I were designing this tapestry today, there might be some items hanging along the bottom to comment on where we get our "facts" and how they are reinforced by the social echo chamber so many of us live in. If we knew more people who were not exactly like us, it would be easier to think of them as individual human beings, and much more difficult to think of them as representatives of homogenous groups, statistics, or opponents who deserve what they get.

Kathy Weber has been interested in the fiber arts from the moment she first held needle and thread as a two-year-old. In more recent years, most of her learning has come through the Weavers' Guild of Rochester or through its instructional arm, the Weaving and Fiber Arts Center. Kathy Weber began weaving in 2006. After beginning weaving, she quickly branched out into an intensive study of Japanese shibori dyeing and other textile techniques with Jane Bartlett and John Marshall, selling her work at venues such as Jane Ellen's Boutique, the Memorial Art Gallery Store, MAG Clothesline Shows, and yearly WGR Sales. Kathy continues to study weaving with Joyce Robards and has studied tapestry with Mary McMahon, Connie Lippert, Ruth Manning, and Rebecca Metzoff. Kathy Weber's work has been seen in local and national shows.

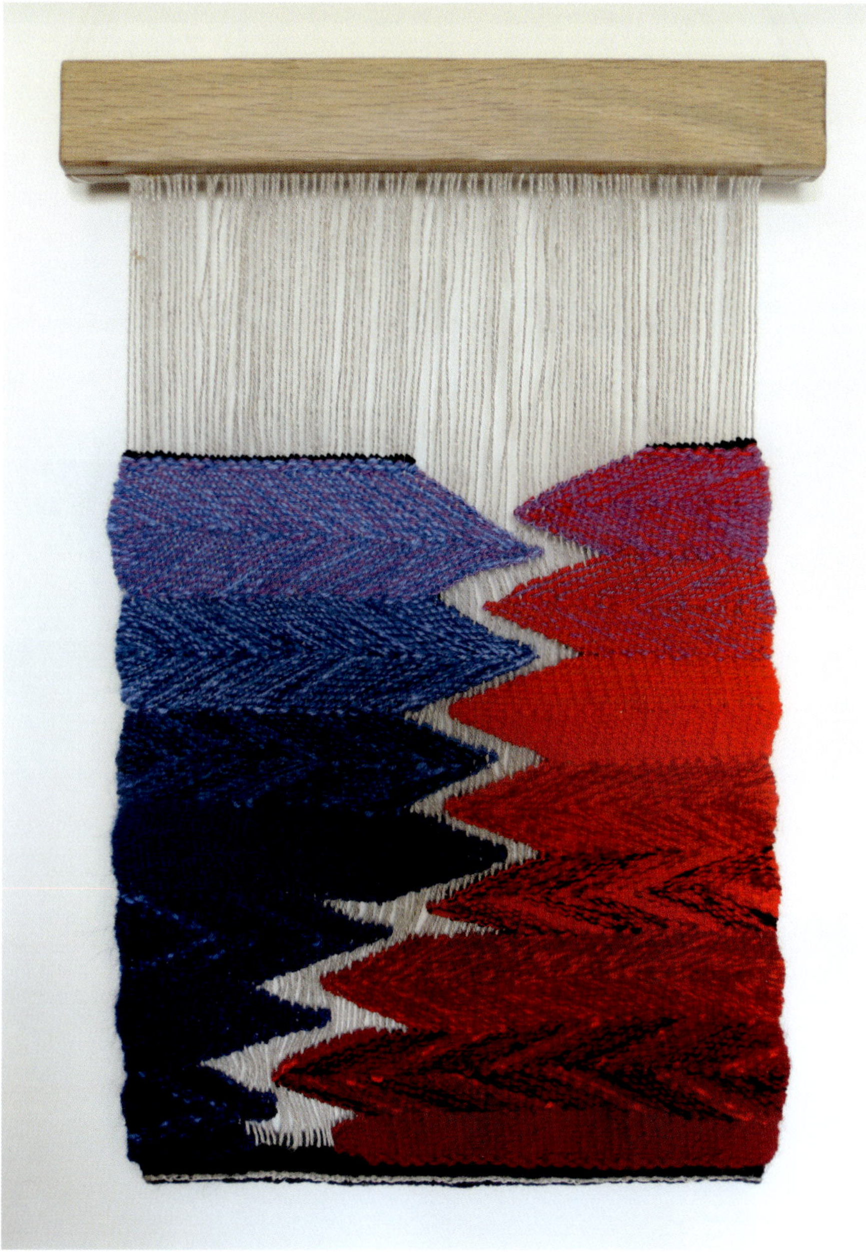

Wendy R. Weiss
Resist

2016 / Cotton dyed with natural dyes: madder root (red), weld (yellow), and ferrous fermentation vat (black) / 21.5 x 40"

Acts of resistance are documented in the literature about life in the Polish ghettos and concentration camps of World War II. I honor the individuals who had the courage to act morally in the face of life-threatening and deadly conditions with the weaving titled *Resist*. The word continues to resonate today.

Wendy Weiss is an independent artist and weaver. Political and social dynamics have informed her individual work and her collaborative work with Jay Kreimer. World War II and the first use of nuclear weapons motivated a series of large weavings and a sculpture called *The Pentagon Project*. She uses natural dyes that she cultivates and collects locally, and teaches workshops on natural dye and warp ikat at various crafts schools nationally and internationally.

She is a past recipient of two Nebraska Arts Council Artist Fellowships, as well as a Winterthur residential fellowship. Her work has been exhibited in solo and group shows in North America, Europe, and Asia. She served on the board of the Textile Society of America, beginning a four-year term in 2014 as communications director. Her current responsibility is senior editor.

CONNECT

https://wendyweiss.org/
https://www.facebook.com/wrweiss
Instagram: @wendyrweiss

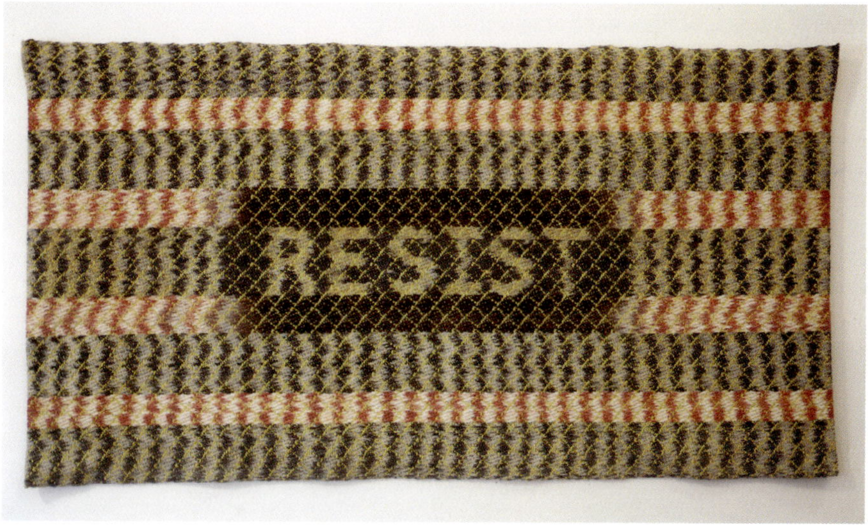
RESIST

Emma Werowinski

Sending Critique Poem Tea Towels to Senators

2018 / Cotton, linen, embroidery thread, four USPS Priority Mail packages, four printed letters / each towel measures 31 x 16"

Recent critiques of the United States government have increasingly called Congress, especially the Senate, "broken." If something is broken, how do we fix it? These four handwoven tea towel designs are each embroidered with poems full of fixing metaphors. They are objects made to do a job (to clean with), yet are often only hung on the wall as decoration, too pretty to use. Duplicates of each design were sent via Priority Mail to four senators (two Democrats and two Republicans) at their Washington, DC offices in early July 2018. A note included in each package read, "This package contains a cotton/linen tea towel embroidered with a poem. It is a gift, because I believe that poems are meant to be shared, and that this poem is applicable to you in your work within the United States Senate." It is important to note that, according to Senate Rule 35.1(a), senators are not allowed to accept gifts from private citizens valued at more than fifty dollars. I received no responses.

Emma Werowinski loves drawing flowcharts, reading pedantic government manuals, deciphering organizational power structures, and scheming about ways for artists to work within government. Her current artistic and research practice is an investigation, visualization, and communication of government structures and processes that are typically contained in difficult-to-access language. She thinks a lot about metaphors like "the fabric of the city" and believes that textiles have the power to act as models of complex abstract systems normally explained only with words or flowcharts. She graduated in 2018 from Rhode Island School of Design, where she studied textiles.

CONNECT

www.emmawerowinski.com
Instagram: @crocbabe.govt

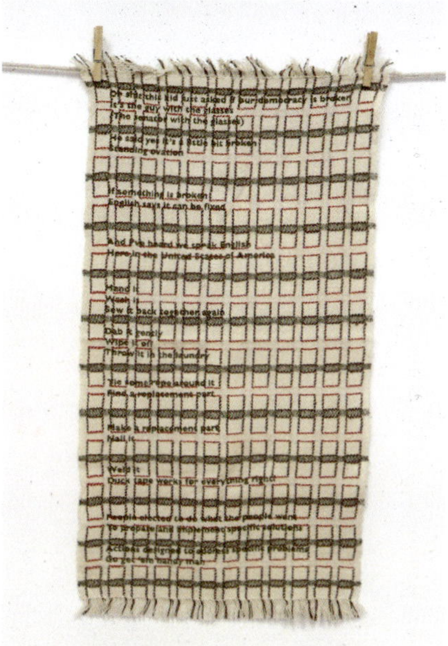
It's the guy with the glasses
(The senator with the glasses)
He said yes it's a little bit broken
Standing ovation
If something is broken
English says it can be fixed
And I've heard we speak English
Here in the United States of America
Mend it
Wash it
Sew it back together again
Dab it gently
Wipe it off
Throw it in the laundry
Tie some rope around it
Find a replacement part
Make a replacement part
Nail it
Weld it
Duck tape works for everything right?
Go get 'em handy man

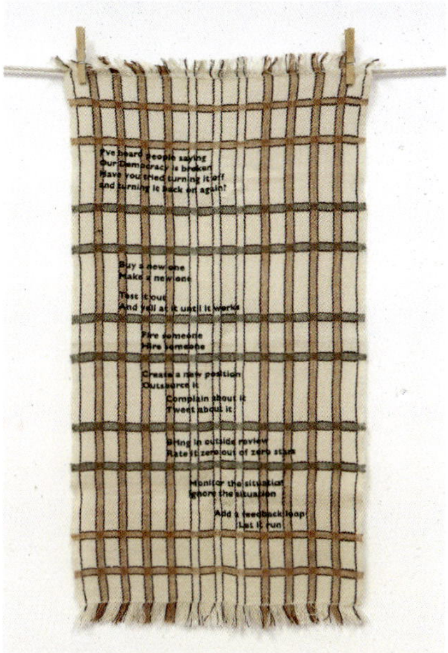
I've heard people saying
Our Democracy is broken
Have you tried turning it off
and turning it back on again?
Buy a new one
Make a new one
Test it out
And yell at it until it works
Fire someone
Hire someone
Create a new position
Outsource it
Complain about it
Tweet about it
Bring in outside review
Rate it zero out of zero stars
Monitor the situation
Ignore the situation
Add a feedback loop
Let it run

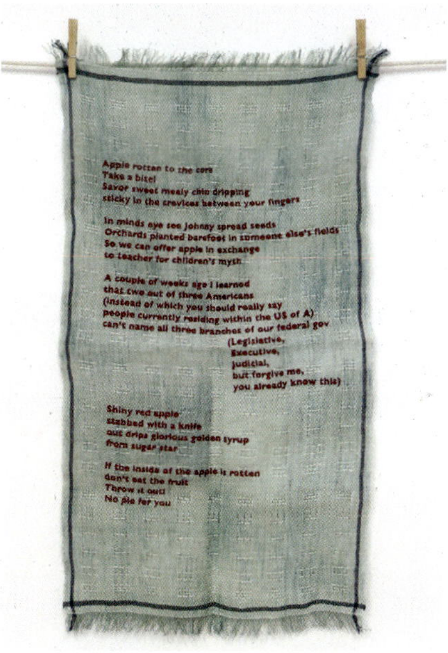
Apple rotten to the core
Take a bite!
Savor sweet mealy chin dripping
sticky in the crevices between your fingers
In minds eye see Johnny spread seeds
Orchards planted barefoot in someone else's fields
So we can offer apple in exchange
to teacher for children's myth
A couple of weeks ago I learned
that two out of three Americans
(instead of which you should really say
people currently residing within the US of A)
can't name all three branches of our federal gov
(Legislative,
Executive,
Judicial,
but forgive me,
you already know this)
Shiny red apple
stabbed with a knife
out drips glorious golden syrup
from sugar star
If the inside of the apple is rotten
don't eat the fruit
Throw it out!
No pie for you

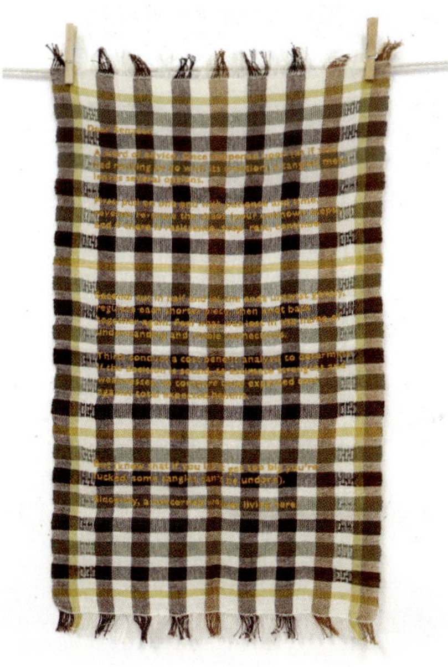

How to Fix a System #1

Oh shit this kid just asked if our democracy is broken
It's the guy with the glasses
(The senator with the glasses)
He said yes it's a little bit broken
Standing ovation

If something is broken
English says it can be fixed
And I've heard we speak English
Here in the United States of America

Mend it
Wash it
Sew it back together again

Dab it gently
Wipe it off
Throw it in the laundry

Tie some rope around it
Find a replacement part
Make a replacement part

Nail it
Weld it
Duck tape works for everything right?

People elected to do what the people want
To prepare and implement specific solutions
Actions designed to address specific problems
Go get 'em handy man

How to Fix a System #2

I've heard people saying
Our Democracy is broken
Have you tried turning it off
and turning it back on again?

Buy a new one
Make a new one
Test it out
And yell at it until it works

Fire someone
Hire someone
Create a new position
Outsource it

Complain about it
Tweet about it
Bring in outside review
Rate it zero out of zero stars

Monitor the situation
Ignore the situation
Add a feedback loop
Let it run

Rotten Apple

Apple rotten to the core
Take a bite!
Savor sweet mealy chin dripping
Sticky in the crevices between your fingers

In minds eye see Johnny spread seeds
Orchards planted barefoot in someone else's fields
So we can offer apple in exchange
To teacher for children's myth

A couple of weeks ago I learned
That two out of three Americans
(instead of which you should really say
people currently residing with the US of A)
can't name all three branches of our federal government
(Legislative,
Executive,
Judicial,
but forgive me,
you already know this)

Shiny red apple
stabbed with a knife
out drips glorious golden syrup
from sugar star

If the inside of the apple is rotten
don't eat the fruit
Throw it out!
No pie for you

What to do with a tangled mess

Dear Senator,

A word of advice. Once happened upon (as if you had nothing to do with its creation) a tangled mess leaves several options.

First: pull on one end with patience and time, reverse, re-trace the chaos (your unknown steps), and if there is resistance, stop, rest, continue.

Second: cut in half and let the ends untwist gently, regulate each shorter piece, then knot back together again. Feel what was lost in the name of understanding and visible connections.

Third: conduct a cost benefit analysis to determine if the decision is sound, to estimate strengths and weaknesses, to compare total expected cost against total expected benefit.

But (know that if you let it get too big you're fucked, some tangles can't be undone).

Sincerely, a concerned weaver living here.

Stephen L. Wilson
Rise Up I

2017 / Polyester twill with polyester embroidery floss, PVC blocks / 36 x 36"

An exploration of appropriation, both in medium and in imagery, is inherent in *Rise Up I*. Appropriation is prevalent throughout modern American history, recognized in a multitude of ways from fine art to protest activism. Stephen continues this exploration by appropriating pop art, historical icons, and gender-signifying symbols, and reimagining them through thread and fabric. He aims to show ways in which the medium can intentionally further the message. In Wilson's appropriation, embroidery is meaningful to achieve this end, due to its traditionally female lineage and associations with second-wave feminist movements.

Rise Up I specifically is inspired by a World War II poster (*We Can Do It!* by J. Howard Miller, 1942) created originally to promote both male and female workers in the Westinghouse factory. The poster later became a symbol of the women's labor movement and is now associated with, and often called, *Rosie the Riveter*. Stephen wanted to build on the deep history of this iconic image, still resonating today, while giving it a contemporary twist. To him, the purple hair and tattooed skin represent self-ownership and expression of identity.

Based in Charlotte, North Carolina, Stephen Wilson is a conceptual multimedia artist working predominately in fabric and thread. As a fine artist, he is deeply interested in the intersection of traditional craft and contemporary culture. Stephen aims to evoke questions about embroidery as a fine art medium by placing textiles and thread in conversation with established art-making processes.

His work is found in galleries, museums, and private collections worldwide. His public art installation *Americana*, an 8-by-23.5-foot larger-than-life "patchwork quilt," was displayed at Lincoln Center in New York and the Blumenthal Performing Arts Center in Charlotte, NC. Stephen's work was also acquired internationally by the National Gallery of Art (Sofia, Bulgaria), Min Art Museum (Guadalajara, Mexico), and the Brunello Cucinelli headquarters (Solomeo, Italy). He has been featured in numerous fine art and popular media such as *Town & Country*, *Huffington Post*, and *Art Hive*.

CONNECT

www.stephenwilsonstudio.com
Instagram: @stephenwilsonstudio

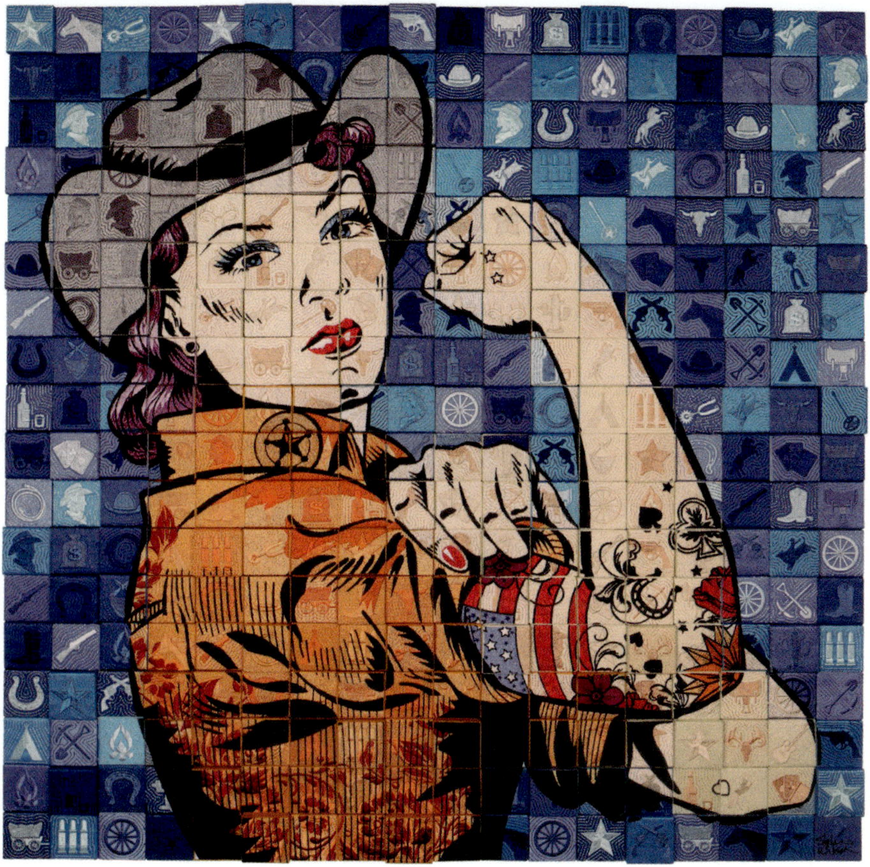

Afterword: Spinning Material Messages

Sarah Parrish, PhD

Enough! Organize. Resist. Break the glass ceiling, stab out stereotypes, and insert mythological adage of virtuous womanhood (here). These are a few of the many messages that march across the walls of *Crafting Democracy: Fiber Arts and Activism* like so many picket signs. Roughly three-quarters of the works on display contain writing of some kind, and many of these inscriptions are calls to action. Surrounding the visitor, they collectively create an atmosphere of protest, recalling the gatherings of Occupy Wall Street in 2011, the Black Lives Matter movement in 2014, and the Women's Marches of 2017, among other recent rallies. The viewer becomes a participant, compelled to take a stand on issues ranging from racism to feminism to marriage equality.

It is perhaps unsurprising that so many of the artists in *Crafting Democracy* have chosen to promote their causes through either the written word or recognizable imagery. Activists endeavor to change their world by raising awareness, and direct language ensures they are readily understood by the public. Language also creates continuity with other political modes of address. However, the reasons why artists find fiber such an appropriate medium for their messages are more complex. The authors of this volume have considered this question from diverse angles, including fiber's gendered associations, its DIY accessibility, and its role in preserving family history. Yet another answer circles back to the issue of language and its intimate relationship to fiber. The words *text* and *textile* share a common root in the Latin *textere*, to weave. Fiber arts, then, share the written word's capacity for communication.

Functioning as a language in its own right, fiber expresses direct material messages that do not require translation. Every human being comes into contact with fabric daily in the form of clothing, bedding, or furnishings, and intuitively understands its connotations of warmth, labor, and heritage. Textiles therefore possess a unique ability to speak universally, while retaining the authentic dialect of their source (counter)-culture. In a political landscape that is increasingly demarcated by borders and walls, the cross-cultural language of thread becomes more essential than ever.

For the artists in *Crafting Democracy: Fiber Arts and Activism*, the medium of fiber reinforces the meaning behind written slogans or pictorial symbols. Each artwork essentially speaks twice—once through its content, and again through its material. The result is the visual equivalent of a shout. Each message is inseparable from fibers that form it, and traditional distinctions between figure and ground, image and caption dissolve into a single powerful statement. Answer the call of these stitched slogans, and don't mourn. Run for prez! In the fibers of this exhibition, love wins.

Sarah Parrish, PhD, is program coordinator and assistant professor of art history at Plymouth State University, New Hampshire, where her research focuses on issues of embodiment, gender, and cultural appropriation in contemporary fiber art.

Acknowledgments

Because the planning and execution of an exhibit is collaborative in nature, we would like to make particular mention of those who quite literally helped bring this show to life. While a complete list of acknowledgments is included in the exhibit and on our website (craftingdemocracy.com), we want to acknowledge here the generous support of the Farash Foundation, which believed in the vision of this exhibit and book from the beginning. Their generosity is the keystone to this years-long project. In addition, the project received enthusiastic cooperation and appreciated support from members of the exhibits staff of the Central Library of Rochester & Monroe County: Corinne Clar, senior graphic designer; Alicia Gunther, librarian; Nanci Nugent, librarian, Arts and Literature Division. The exhibition is bolstered by the essay in this book which gave the following scholars, curators, and practitioners opportunities shared their experience, voice, and vision: Betty M. Bayer, professor of Women's Studies at Hobart and William Smith Colleges, and past president of the Board of Directors of the National Women's Hall of Fame; Kate Bonansinga, director of the School of Art, University of Cincinnati; Beth McLaughlin, chief curator of exhibitions and collections at Fuller Craft Museum in Massachusetts; Alena Amato Ruggerio, professor of communication at Southern Oregon University; Margo Smith, cofounder of the Kudzu Project, based in central Virginia; and Sarah Parrish, assistant professor of art history at Plymouth State University in New Hampshire.

We are grateful to the funding support from the Friends & Foundation of the Rochester Public Library, and RIT's Museum Studies Program and the School of Communication.

We extend our gratitude to RIT Press and its director, Bruce Austin, for believing that this exhibit should be immortalized in book form; and we extend special appreciation to RIT Press managing editor, Molly Cort, for shepherding this project through to completion without a hitch; to designer, Marnie Soom, for her design brilliance; and to copyeditor, Amy Mantell, for her sharp eye and gift with words.

Through this exhibition and the associated activities during its tenure, viewers are offered a link to the past, but also to the present and future. We are grateful to our colleagues within the College of Liberal Arts at RIT, who've been an enthusiastic support system. We are grateful to our collaborators—Melissa Manczuk, Mary Fraser, Carol Moldt, Diane Premo, Jennifer Cesare, and Brandon Fess, librarians at the Central Library of Rochester & Monroe County—who have helped us to engage audiences and extend the exhibition experience beyond the gallery walls.

Finally, we thank the artists who submitted their work in response to our call for submissions. We were overwhelmed with the international response from artists, crafts people, and makers who explore how the making of art and the creation of material objects can unite, divide, unsettle, and uplift those who live in the United States. We thank each and every one of you for your commitment to making visible the ways in which fiber can be employed as a tool to build community through participatory action and to craft democracy.

Image Credits

16	C.J. Lind
18-19	Beth McLaughlin
21	Shannon Downey
25	Gary Connaughton
29-31	Tony Walsh
34, 36	Tom Cogill
41	Allyson D. Allen
43	Ellis Angel
45	Christy Bailey
47	Deb J. Berkebile
49	Eva Camacho-Sanchez
51	Margaret A. Cherre
53	Laura Wulf
55	Sonja Dahl
57	Elizabeth Lamark
59	Katrina L. Herron Gendreau
61	Wilson Graham
63	Yvonne Fuchs
65	Jessica Lacher-Feldman
67-69	Myoung Studio
71	Tina MacIntyre-Yee
73	Beth Ann MacVittie
75	Katrina Majkut
77	Elizabeth Lamark
79	Kayla Mattes
81	Joetta Maue
83	Nanci Nugent
85	Alfonse Pagano
87	Wayne Smith
89	Jessica M. Skultety
91, 93	Adrienne Sloane
95-97	Jill St. Coeur
99	Aaron Paden
101	Melanie Tuazon
103	Melita A. Gill
105	Wendy R. Weiss
107	Emma Werowinski
111	Stephen L. Wilson

Index

Page locators in *italics* indicate photographs or their captions.

abolitionist movement, 3–4
AIDS Memorial Quilt, 24
Allen, Allyson D., 40–41
Amelon, Jane, 25–26
American Craft Council, 27
Angel, Ellis, 42–43
Anthony, Susan B., 3, 12, 50, 64, 70
art museums, role of, 16–17, 20
art quilts, 22
artistic media, hierarchy of, 9
artistic value, measure of, 20
autonomy, 23

Badass Cross Stitch, *21*
Bailey, Christy, 44–45
Battered Offenders Self-Help Group, 25–26
Bayer, Betty M., 1
Berkebile, Deb J., 46–47
Black Doll in Plaid Dress (Nugent), 82, *83*
Black Lives Matter movement, 113
blankets, 28, *30*
Bonansinga, Kate, 27–31
Bowen, Jeanine, 100
Break the Glass Ceiling (St. Coeur), 94, *95*
Bystander (Lee), 66, *67–69*

Camacho-Sanchez, Eva, 48–49
Central Library of Rochester & Monroe County, 4, 5, 82, 115, 116
Charleston Emanuel AME Church, 33
Charlottesville, Virginia, 32
Cherre, Margaret A., 50–51
citizenship status, 4–5
civil rights movement, 33
Civil War, 23, 32–33
Cleaning America (Bailey), 44, *45*
Clinton, Hillary, 3, 12, 52, *53*, 94
Clutterbuck-Cook, Anna J., 52–53
coding, crafting compared to, 7–8
collaboration, 23, 56–57, 100
Color, Gender, Power, Order (Hesh), 60, *61*
Confederate statues, 32–37, *34*, *36*
Contemporary Arts Center (CAC; Cincinnati, Ohio), 27–28, *28–29*, *31*
Conway, Kellyanne, 98, *99*
Cotton Sophisticate (Kimber), 62, *63*
Coyle, Kat, 7, 17n3
craft
- as activism, 6–9
- meaning of, 1
- role of, 2, 4

Crafting Dissent: Handicraft as Protest from the American Revolution to the Pussyhats (Mandell), 3, 14, 76
craftivism
- after 2016 presidential election, 15
- artistic value and, 20

capturing spirit of, 20–21
definition of, 6
in institutional settings, 17
Crawley, Aleeda, 100
crochet
Which Hat Is Which? Pussy Hat, the Original Pussyhat, Dunce Cap, Drumpf Hat, Make America Great Again Hat (Mandell), *77*
cross-stitch
Color, Gender, Power, Order (Hesh), 60, *61*
Cross-Stitch and Yarn Marker Commemorating the First Frederick Douglass Family House in Rochester, New York (Flaherty, Horowitz, Mandell, Schmuecker, and Sovern), 56, *57*
DIY Counted Cross-Stitch Woman Card Kit (Majkut), 74, *75*
Female Inheritance (Gendreau), 58, *59*
Persistent Stitches I (Clutterbuck-Cook), 52, *53*
Cross-Stitch and Yarn Marker Commemorating the First Frederick Douglass Family House in Rochester, New York (Flaherty, Horowitz, Mandell, Schmuecker, and Sovern), 56, *57*
Cunningham, Joe, 22

Dahl, Sonja, 54–55
Decker, Juilee, 2–5, 6–9
democracy/democratization
AIDS Memorial Quilt and, 24
arts and crafts and, 27
participation in, 4–5
DIY Counted Cross-Stitch Woman Card Kit (Majkut), 74, *75*
domestic violence, 25–26
Don't Mourn, Organize (Angel), 42, *43*
Douglass, Anna, 56–57
Douglass, Frederick, 3, 12, 50, 56–57
dyeing
Cotton Sophisticate (Kimber), 62, *63*
Enough (Camacho-Sanchez), 48, *49*
Resist (Weiss), 104, *105*
Still Dreaming of Equality II (Berkebile), 46, *47*

embroidery, 12, 15
Female Inheritance (Gendreau), 58, *59*
Mother and Child (Maue), 80, *81*
Our War Cry (Lacher-Feldman), 64, *65*
Persistent Stitches I (Clutterbuck-Cook), 52, *53*
Rise Up I (Wilson), 110, *111*
Sending Critique Poem Tea Towels to Senators (Werowinski), 106, *107*
Un-word of the Year (Suprenant), 98, *99*
empowerment, 23–24
Enough (Camacho-Sanchez), 48, *49*
Equal Pay for Equal Work (St. Coeur), 94, *97*
equality, 5, 17, 48, 50, 86, 113
Eyes on the Lies: 100 Days of Fictionary (Sloane), 92, *93*

Fader, Sarah, 100
family separations, 2
felt
Enough (Camacho-Sanchez), 48, *49*
Female Inheritance (Herron Gendreau), 58, *59*
fiber
as activist medium, 1, 2–3, 5, 9, 116
language and, 113–114
as platform for expression, 2–3
spinning, 13–14
symbolic meaning of, 13–14
figures, three-dimensional
Black Doll in Plaid Dress (Nugent), 82, *83*
Bystander (Lee), 66, *67–69*
flags
Cleaning America (Bailey), 44, *45*
#TAKEAKNEE, 40, *41*
Twelve Plus One (Pagano), 84, *85*
Unraveling, The (Sloane), 90, *91*
Flaherty, Alison, 56–57
flash installations, *36*
Fuller Craft Museum, 17, *18–19*, 20–21, 88, 115

Games People Play (Sloane), 92, *93*
gender, art quilting and, 22–26
Greer, Betsy, 6
gun violence, 48–49

Harold Hacker Hall, iv, 4
Hear Our Voice (Skultety), 88, *89*
Herron Gendreau, Katrina L., 58–59
Hesh, Suzanne, 60–61
Hinton, Ashley, 100
Holocaust, 10, 12
hope, 2, 4, 52, 70
Horowitz, Carin, 56–57

identity politics, 4, 58
immigration, 16, 50, 102

Jordan, Karin, 100
Just Rewards (St. Coeur), 94, *95–97*

Kimber, Chawne M., 62–63
King, Martin Luther, Jr., 46
KKK, 32, 76, *77*
knitting
- compared to coding, 7–8
- *Unraveling, The* (Sloane), 90, *91*
- *Written on My Chest* (Liano), 70, *71*

Kudzu Project, 32–37, *34–35*, *36*

Lacher-Feldman, Jessica, 64–65
Lee, June, 66–69
Liano, Betsy, 70–71
Lost Cause mythology, 33
Love Wins! (Pellman), 86, *87*

MacVittie, Beth Ann, 72–73
Majkut, Katrina, 74–75
Mandell, Hinda, 2–5, 7n4, 10–14, 56–57, 76–77
marriage equality, 86–87, 113
Marzio, Peter, 27, 31
Mattes, Kayla, 78–79
Maue, Joetta, 80–81
McLaughlin, Beth C., 15–21
mixed media
- *Don't Mourn, Organize* (Angel), 42, *43*

Mother and Child (Maue), 80, *81*

nasty women, 14, 76, 86
Nevertheless She Persisted (MacVittie), 72, *73*
Nugent, Nanci, 82–83, 115

Occupy Wall Street, 113
Olander, Alyson, 100
open-source patterns, 7
Our War Cry (Lacher-Feldman), 64, *65*

Pagano, Alfonse, 84–85
Parrish, Sarah, 114–115
participation
- audience, 20
- democratic, 4–5
- fostering of, 8

Patel, Krishma, 100
patterns, 6, 7–9, 11, 22, 48, 50, 70
Pellman, Kathryn, 86–87
Persistent Stitches I (Clutterbuck-Cook), 52, *53*
Persisterhood, 12
polarization, 4
presidential election of 2016, 1, 3, 4, 6, 11–12, 14, 15–16, 50, 52, 70, 72, 88
presidential inauguration, 7, 15, 98
Pussyhat Project, 7, 12, 15–16, 17, 20–21, 33, 35, 64

Quaal, Melissa, 100
quilting
- #TAKEAKNEE, 40, *41*
- *Cotton Sophisticate* (Kimber), 62, *63*
- *Don't Mourn, Organize* (Angel), 42, *43*
- *Eyes on the Lies: 100 Days of Fictionary* (Sloane), 92, *93*
- *Games People Play* (Sloane), 92, *93*
- gender and injustice and, 22–26

Hear Our Voice (Skultety), 88, *89*
Know Their Names: Groper Word Search (Sloane), 92, *93*
Love Wins! (Pellman), 86, *87*
Persistent Stitches I (Clutterbuck-Cook), 52, *53*
Seven Dirty Words: CDC Anagram (Sloane), 92, *93*
Still Dreaming of Equality II (Berkebile), 46, *47*
Un-word of the Year (Suprenant), 98, *99*
What Did Ming Miss? (Suprenant), 98
Women's Work (Tuazon), 100, *101*

race issues/racism, 23–24, 50
Rapid Response Collection (Victoria and Albert Museum), 16
Reagan administration, 24
refugee resettlement, 16
Reiter, Michelle, 100
resilience, 4
Resist (Weiss), 104, *105*
Revolution in the Making: The Pussyhat Project (Fuller Craft Museum), 17, *18–19*, 20–21
Rise Up I (Wilson), 110, *111*
Robinson, Virginia, 100
Rosie the Riveter, 110
rug hooking, 94, *95–97*
Ruggerio, Alena Amato, 22–26
Run for Prez (St. Coeur), 94, *96*
Rush to Relics (Pagano), *85*

Schmuecker, Penny, 56–57
Secession Quilt (Cook), 23
Sending Critique Poem Tea Towels to Senators (Werowinski), 106, *107*, 108–109
share culture, 7
Skultety, Jessica M., 88–89
Sloane, Adrienne, 90–91, 92–93
Smith, Margo, 32–37
source code, 7–8
Sovern, Elizabeth, 56–57
spinning fiber, 13–14
St. Coeur, Jill, 94–95
State of the Union (Weber), 102, *103*
Still Dreaming of Equality II (Berkebile), 46, *47*
suffrage movement, 3–4, 6, 52, *53*, 70
Suh, Krista, 7, 17n3
Sullivan, Anne, 100
Suprenant, Kathy A., 98–99
Syjuco, Stephanie, 6–7

tactility, 9
tailoring business, 10–11
#TAKEAKNEE, 40, *41*
textiles, as models of complex systems, 1
Trump, Donald J., 3, 11, 15, *77*, 78, *79*, 92, 94
Tuazon, Melanie, 100–101
Twelve Plus One (Pagano), 84, *85*

UMP (Mattes), 78, *79*
Unite the Right rally (Charlottesville, Virginia), 32
Unraveled: Challenging Textile Traditions (CAC exhibition), 27–28, *28–31*, 30–31
Unraveling, The (Sloane), 90, *91*
Un-word of the Year (Suprenant), 98, *99*

Victoria and Albert Museum, 15–16
voting rights, 50

Warren, Elizabeth, 72
We Can Do It! (Miller), 110
weaving
Don't Mourn, Organize (Angel), 42, *43*
Nevertheless She Persisted (MacVittie), 72, *73*
Resist (Weiss), 104, *105*
Sending Critique Poem Tea Towels to Senators (Werowinski), 106, *107*
State of the Union (Weber), 102, *103*
UMP (Mattes), *79*
Whitework: Race Traitor (Dahl), 54, *55*
Will It Ever End (Cherre), 50, *51*

Weber, Kathy J., 102–103
Weiss, Wendy R., 104–105
Werowinski, Emma, 106–109
What Did Ming Miss? (Suprenant), 98
Which Hat Is Which? Pussy Hat, the Original Pussyhat, Dunce Cap, Drumpf Hat, Make America Great Again Hat (Mandell), 76, *77*
Whitework: Race Traitor (Dahl), 54, *55*
Wilkin, Kitty, 100
Will It Ever End (Cherre), 50, *51*
Wilson, Stephen L., 110–111
Women's March on Washington, 7, 15, 17, 33, 35, 42–43, 64, 72, 76, 88, 113
Women's Work (Tuazon), 100, *101*
Written on My Chest (Liano), 70, *71*

yarn intervention, 12